Pioneering in Territorial Silver City

Henry (Harry) Boyar Ailman. (Ailman Scrapbook)

Pioneering in Territorial Silver City

H. B. AILMAN'S RECOLLECTIONS
OF SILVER CITY
AND THE SOUTHWEST, 1871–1892

Edited and Annotated by
Helen J. Lundwall

Published in cooperation with the
Historical Society of New Mexico

Cartography by Ralph Fisher and M. L. Lundwall
Illustrations by M. L. Lundwall

University of New Mexico Press
Albuquerque

Library of Congress Cataloging in Publication Data

Ailman, Harry B., 1845–1938.
   Pioneering in territorial Silver City.

   Bibliography: p.
   Includes index.
   1. Ailman, Harry B. 1845–1938. 2. Silver City
Region (N.M.)—History. 3. Silver mines and mining—
New Mexico—Silver City Region—History. 4. Frontier
and pioneer life—New Mexico—Silver City Region.
5. Pioneers—New Mexico—Silver City Region—Biography.
6. Silver City Region (N.M.)—Biography. I. Lundwall,
Helen J., 1926–   . II. Title.
F804.S58A37   1983   978.9′692   83–1314
ISBN 0–8263–0685–3
ISBN 0–8263–0686–1 (pbk.)

Contents

Illustrations

Maps

Foreword

The Historical Society of New Mexico, in cooperation with the University of New Mexico Press, is pleased to copublish this memoir of Harry B. Ailman (1845–1938), which is set in the southwestern part of our state during the Territorial era. Ailman came to Silver City just fourteen months after its founding; for the next twenty years he was part of the town's growth and prosperity—first in mining and then in commerce and banking. Though he left in the 1890s, his presence endures in two monuments: in the Ailman House, the first of a number of elegant Victorian homes erected in Silver City during the prosperous 1880s, and which is today the fine Silver City Museum; in this memoir, which brings to life in fascinating detail the bygone period of hard luck mining and the even harder knock, laissez-faire, capitalism of the Gilded Age.

Pioneering in Territorial Silver City: H. B. Ailman's Recollections of Silver City and the Southwest, 1871–1892 is the fourth volume in a copublication series between the Historical Society and the University of New Mexico Press. The appearance of this book nearly a century after Ailman made the original journal entries is fulfillment of one of the purposes of the series—to publish works on New Mexico history, emphasizing those areas and topics not covered previously.

The history of southern New Mexico, and in particular its social and economic development, is too often slighted in favor of events elsewhere in the state. Yet as shown by Darlis Miller in *The California Column in New Mexico*—the third volume in this series—mining and commerce in that area during the Territorial period was a compelling human drama. Ailman's recollections are an authentic voice of a man who rose from pushing a wheelbarrow to running a bank; his account preserves the details of daily life in mining camps—from cooking to geology—as well as of the rise and collapse of a small businessman.

Helen J. Lundwall, librarian at the Silver City Public Library, has been a true historian-detective in editing and annotating this volume. Her notes carefully and dispassionately reconstruct the background of the people, places, and events that Ailman introduces. In addition to numerous photographs of the period—many taken from Ailman's scrapbook—she has included maps and sketches prepared especially for the book by her husband. These illustrations enhance the lively and engaging text left by Harry B. Ailman.

The publication of this book enables the Historical Society to continue fulfilling one of the roles assigned to it by the Board of Directors—to increase the research and writing of New Mexico history by making available original and reliable contributions to our state's past development. The partnership with the University of New Mexico Press makes possible the publication of books which contribute to an understanding and appreciation of our regional culture and its historic development.

The 1982 officers and directors are: *Officers:* Albert H. Schroeder, President; John P. Conron, Vice President; Austin Hoover, 2nd Vice President; Hedy M. Dunn, Secretary; and Charles Bennett, Treasurer. *Directors:* Thomas E. Chavez,

Timothy Cornish, Hobart Durham, Octavia Fellin, Myra Ellen Jenkins, Loraine Lavender, William Lock, Luther L. Lyon, Morgan Nelson, Jacquelyn Otero, Nancy Robertson, Joe W. Stein, Spencer Wilson, and Stephen Zimmer.

John P. Conron, Chairman
Publications Committee
Historical Society of New Mexico

Preface

Harry Ailman (1845–1938), like thousands of other adventurous young men, came west to seek his fortune. When he arrived in Grant County, New Mexico, in 1871, he found little to indicate that this southwestern corner of the territory was soon to play a leading role in the development of the mining industry in New Mexico. At that time the copper mines at Santa Rita were abandoned and the gold placers at Pinos Altos were half-deserted for lack of water. The value of recently discovered silver deposits at Ralston and Silver City had not yet been established. Hostile Apaches roamed the countryside, ambushing unwary prospectors and raiding the small, scattered settlements.

Harry lived in Grant County for twenty-one years. During this time he saw the county develop from a wilderness into a flourishing area caught up in the excitement of a mining boom. Gold, silver, and copper were discovered in abundance, and prospectors roamed the hills seeking the elusive bonanza. Mining claims were located in every direction, and hastily-built camps sprang up around each new discovery. By 1883 Grant County had become the leading producer of precious metals in the territory and was often referred to as "the treasure vault of New Mexico."

After prospecting for several years with little success, Harry and a partner, Henry Meredith, struck it rich. Their discovery, the Naiad Queen, turned out to be the best producing silver mine in Georgetown. Determination and hard work earned Harry many years of prosperity, first as a Georgetown miner, and later as a Silver City merchant and banker. Although his sojourn in New Mexico ended in misfortune, he always remembered those years as the most exciting and happiest time of his life.

In 1890 Harry wrote an account of his trek to New Mexico, following closely the diary in which he kept a day by day record of the journey. Many years later, after retiring from an active life, he completed his memoirs. Each page was carefully written in longhand and pasted in a large scrapbook, along with many of the photographs included in this book. In telling this story of his personal life and fortunes, he used letters, business papers, and notes to aid a remarkably keen memory. His recollections present a reliable, firsthand account of events that shaped the early development of southwestern New Mexico and introduce many of the prominent local personalities of that period.

In editing this manuscript, every effort has been made to maintain Harry's style and individuality throughout the story. Punctuation, paragraphing, and capitalization have been added for easier reading. A small amount of irrelevant or repetitious material has been deleted. Where certain passages from the original diaries of the trip to New Mexico were found to be more descriptive or detailed, they were added. The footnotes are intended to verify his statements or supply additional information that might interest the reader.

Ailman's given name was actually Henry, but he was known to family, friends, and even the newspaper as Harry. This must have been his own preference; therefore, I will also call him Harry throughout this book. This will avoid a certain amount of confusion because his partner, Hartford M. Meredith, was known as Henry.

I am particularly grateful to Harry Ailman's daughter, Grace Whittaker, now deceased, who brought the original manuscript to Silver City and gave us permission to edit and publish it. She also provided information about the years after the family left Silver City and made available various diaries and letters.

I am indebted to Mildred A. Ailman, Harry's niece, who first told me about the memoirs and has been helpful in gathering information on the Ailman family. I would also like to thank Harry's granddaughters, Theora M. Adams and Suzanne A. Stokes, for their interest and help.

Very special thanks go to Dottie Hill, my assistant at the Silver City Public Library. Her suggestions were always useful, and the many hours she spent reading the manuscript and compiling the bibliography are greatly appreciated.

Many people have gone out of their way to provide assistance in the preparation of the manuscript. I am especially grateful to the following: Ralph Fisher for his expertise in lettering the maps; Harry Benjamin, curator of the Silver City Museum, for arranging details of publication; Ellen Cline and Susan Berry for help in research and editing; my daughter and son-in-law, Linda and Tom Brake, for listening to progress reports, reading, and advising; Becky Thayer for typing; Helen Curtis and Pat Brandt for proofreading, and Lucille Gray for advice; the staff of the Silver City Public Library for general assistance; Virginia Hunt for proofreading.

Thanks also to the following who furnished information and answered questions: William L. Emery, Clayton, New Mexico; Paul Ton, Aurora, Colorado; Dr. Myra Ellen Jenkins, then of the State Records Center and Archives, Santa

Fe, New Mexico; Darlene E. Hamilton, Seattle Public Library, Seattle, Washington; Annie Gleason, Colorado Springs, Colorado.

I am deeply grateful to my husband, Lee, who created the sketches, drew the maps, solved problems, and accompanied me on many trips in search of information. His sustaining interest, encouragement and understanding have made this book possible.

To all who have expressed interest in these memoirs, I hope you enjoy meeting Harry Ailman as much as I did.

Helen J. Lundwall
Silver City, New Mexico
Summer 1982

1 A Number of Bright Deals

Silver City, New Mexico—June 18, 1890: Owing to an unfavorable turn in the winding up of the affairs of the late firm of Meredith and Ailman, I am detained at home with little to do until the August term of district court. For the benefit of our dear children, my wife requests me to write, from notes I took at the time, a sketch of my overland trip to New Mexico long before the days of railroad into this country. To gratify her request, I will begin by giving an account of my life prior to making that trip.

My father, David Ailman,[1] was born in York County, Pennsylvania, September 15, 1805. Mother, whose maiden name was Amelia Pawling, was born October 5, 1820, in Snyder County near Sealinsgrove. They were married January 24, 1844, and I came on the scene March 19, 1845, in Juniata County, Pennsylvania.

The common schools were nowhere near as thorough and proficient during my parents' school periods as they were when my turn came along. They never got beyond reading, writing, and some arithmetic, and that in the German language. They realized the value of education, however, and determined their children should have the best it was possible to give them. Many an evening Mother spent trying to help us with our lessons. More than one season in the summer, when our help was much needed on the farm, father strained a point to give us the benefit of a summer term at school.

I attended school at McAlisterville Academy and helped my father on the farm until the spring of 1864. Deciding that farm work was a very slow way of getting money to go to school on, at nineteen years of age I set out to find something that paid better. Through the assistance of an acquaintance in the employment of the Pennsylvania Railroad,[2] I got a job in Altoona unloading coal for the locomotives at $1.00 per day. In three or four days I got a chance to go out as extra brakeman on a night freight train at $2.30 per trip.

During the summer I earned enough, over and above my board and washing, to pay my way at the fall term of school at Kishacoquillas Academy in Mifflin County. Following this I received a teaching certificate and secured a job in the Red Rock District school. Terms were four months, beginning November first and ending about March first; salary was $25.00 per month. I boarded at home and walked over two miles across country in all kinds of weather. I was always there and had the stove hot before the children assembled for school to begin at 9:00 A.M.

The term finished, I went back to the railroad for employment, this time to Harrisburg. Owing to the war and consequent scarcity of men, I had little trouble getting a job as brakeman. In six months I was raised to flagman and two and a half years later promoted to a conductorship.

After serving the company for nearly five years, I had helped my father with $1,500 in cash and saved up some $600 besides. I felt I did not want to adopt railroad train running as a life work. There was much of the West still unoccupied, with good land open and only awaiting an occupant. I decided to sever my connection with the railroad and go west. About February 22, 1870, I started out with Kansas as my destination.

I was much impressed by the Kansas prairie as compared to my old home in Pennsylvania with its hilly surface and no end of stones and rocks. Here were unnumbered acres of clean ground, free from stones, still unoccupied although many new homes were springing up. I went one day to a school director's meeting. There, for the first time, I saw women taking part—also voting.[3]

At the end of a month, I decided to see some more of the state. At that time the Kansas Pacific Railroad[4] was completed to the west end of the state and some distance into the territory of Colorado. On this I went as far as Junction City. There a new railroad, called the Missouri, Kansas and Texas,[5] was building south. It was completed almost to the town of Parsons, a line of some seventy or eighty miles. I took this train and landed in Burlington, Coffee County. There was fine prairie land all the way and new settlers in every direction. Here I looked for something to do. There was no manufacturing in this new town, and jobs were scarce. Finally I found a party who wanted a fence built. I tackled this and in a few days had it completed.

It might be well to state here that up to this time in my life I had no capital on which to do any business except to sell my time. As has been shown, this I did to the best advantage within my reach, but it gave me no experience to deal financially with a cold and heartless trading world. My surroundings had all been farming communities and naturally left that impression on me. I now found myself in this lovely-looking country, with unimproved land to be had for a few dollars per acre as compared with the price I was accustomed to back home. On finding an offer of eighty acres at $3.00 per acre, it is not strange that I should bite. This relieved me of $240 of my ready cash, not leaving enough to buy a team and build a cabin.

By this time I had made the acquaintance of two men who claimed to know how to burn brick. It looked as though a demand existed for that product, and it could be sold. The three of us rented a piece of ground that contained what we thought was suitable clay and went to work. As they had no money, I had to put up what cash we needed as we went along. Everything was new, and some were asking one price, some another. I hoped we could make a go of this and was willing to help.

All of us jumped in and mixed mud, molded, and did all the other stunts by hand until we had a kiln of twenty-five thousand bricks. This we sat up day and night to burn. When we opened the kiln, we found to our dismay that the clay was not what we had thought, and the bricks were of inferior quality. Mr. John Robb, one of the partners, proposed that if we were willing to trust him, he would give his note for the amounts due us and try to get us our money back. We accepted and closed up on those terms. He gave me a note for $150, and I look at it now—bright deal number two.

Now free from the brick business, the other partner and I decided to try something else altogether. Canvassing was quite the rage so we picked that for our next venture. Modes of travel at that time were of but two kinds, afoot or horseback, and distance was plenty. Indian ponies were plentiful there so I bought two for fifty dollars apiece. Owing to the fact that many little new homes were being built, we selected bells for the front doors as our line and started out to supply this long felt want. We stuck to it until we landed in Knobnoster, Missouri, making some sales, but not enough to make a go of it, and finding the country had been canvassed to death and few had money to buy.

Feeling I had spent enough time at this, I made a proposition to my partner that he buy me out, and he accepted. This left me with only my ponies on hand. I got them back to Lawrence, and all I could get for them was thirty dollars each. Thus ended deal number three. No gain in the bell business; we just barely came out even.

With no success and my money about gone, I must again try to find something to do. My resolution in regard to railroading, made before I started west, had to be laid aside, and again I applied to the railroad for a job. This time it was the Kansas Pacific, and lo and behold, who should I find as the head man at Lawrence but Robert Gammell, whom I had known as one of the trainmasters on the Pennsylvania Railroad at Altoona. My wants made known, his reply was, "I have no opening here, but will give you a pass to the front and recommend they put you on as brakeman on the construction train." The road was then building west of Kit Carson, Colorado.[6]

I thankfully accepted, and within the next forty-eight hours I arrived at Kit Carson, presented my credentials, and was put on. The town nearest the front was always used as headquarters for construction. This was a tough place, with many being employed and money plentiful. Naturally, the gambling element was attracted, also the feminine end of it. Almost every other building was a saloon where all kinds of whiskey and wine were on tap, and every kind of card game known to the profession ran day and night. With little or no law to settle disputes, what should have been decided by a legally organized court was generally settled with a six-shooter.

I boarded at the hotel, such as it was. Here you were lucky if you got a bed that was not still warm from having just been left by someone else. That, of course, would indicate that you had to straighten it up yourself. This was certainly something for me, a "greenie" with only a few months of western experience, to run into.

The day after my arrival I made my first trip up the line to the front. There I saw something new to me. It was a quarter of beef hanging high up on a telegraph pole in the hot sun. That was their ice chest, and it seemed to work as they practiced it right along. Dry air and no moisture made it solidify where it would have rotted back east.

For untold ages before the coming of the white man, the buffalo range consisted of all the territory lying between the Missouri River and the Rocky Mountains. This was the main source of the Indian's meat supply. The invasion of their range by the Union Pacific Railroad soon convinced these gentlemen that it was only a matter of time until the buffalo would be exterminated and their food supply gone forever. [7] Naturally, this made them exceedingly hostile so that the Union Pacific, the first train through, had all that kind of fighting to contend with. By the time I came on the scene, the Indians were banished back north into Wyoming and the Dakotas and on reservations, and there was no Indian trouble on the Kansas Pacific line. However, this had only been secured a short time before. [8]

I continued my regular runs, hauling ties, iron etc., to the front through July and on into August. Our crews working west, and others working east from Denver, had gotten to the point where there was only ten and a quarter miles of track yet to lay to connect what would be a through line from Kansas City to Denver. The Union Pacific, on their last day, had made a record of laying ten miles in one day, working from both ends. We now were bent on breaking that record. Consequently, at 5:00 A.M. on the 15th of August we were on the job. I never before had a hand in such a rush, although my position as brakeman was quite light compared to those laying the track. That track was laid almost as fast as a man would ordinarily walk; ties, of course, were already in place. At about 3:00 P.M. the gold spike was driven, same as on the Union Pacific main line (this was also U.P. property). This was done with a grand hurrah as we shattered their record.[9]

We had not stopped for anything to eat since breakfast, and all hands were pretty hungry. The crews from Denver loaded up and backed up to their first station, Bijou. We likewise loaded all our boys on and pulled up to the same place where a champagne supper awaited us.[10] Having ravenous appetites from their morning's exercise, the boys partook very freely of the good dinner, including the champagne. In their heated up condition, this did not set very well. I never saw a sicker lot of men. They just lay around everywhere, unable to sit up. The engineer did not dare move the train until the other brakeman and I gave the signal that none of them were under the cars.

We now backed to the nearest siding to clear the way for the first through passenger train over the road. The next day our train crew was converted by the contractor into a passenger crew, and it fell to my lot to ride into Denver on the second through train over the Kansas Pacific Railroad.

The road now completed, the contractor continued to manage the operation of trains until September first when the company accepted the newly completed part and took charge. This brought us a new conductor, by the name of S. E. Hoskins, who kindly consented to retain the balance of the crew and gave me a regular job as brakeman. My run was about half the distance between Kansas City and Denver, or about 325 miles. Our eastern terminus was Ellis.

As this run covered the heart of the buffalo range, it was

nothing strange to occasionally run into a large herd. This would cause the engineer to slow down and toot his whistle. Some buffalo would succeed in crossing the track before the train quite overtook them. Then the rest would do their level best to beat the train and cross, same as the first one. This made it dangerous, for if the engineer should hit one it might throw us off the track.[11]

My career as a brakeman lasted only a little over a month. When the baggageman quit his job I was selected to take his place. This put me in the baggage car permanently. Soon thereafter, going east one morning, we encountered a herd of a hundred or more buffalo on both sides of the track. The engineer tooted the whistle and they started to run. I opened the side door of my car, and there was a big fellow doing his best to get around the train. At that time we always had a half-dozen rifles on hand, with plenty of cartridges for them. I picked one up and let him have it. He tumbled over and stayed where he fell, but we did not stop. That is my buffalo record. I never fired at them again as it was shameful destruction of wild life if you were not in a position to make use of the carcass.[12]

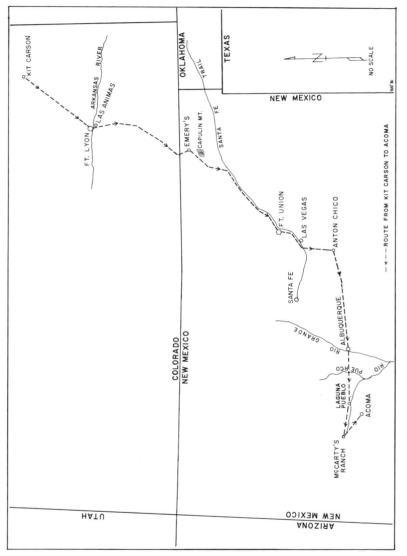

Route of Prospecting Party from Kit Carson to Acoma

2 The Heavens For a Roof and Mother Earth For a Bedstead

In October 1870, I attended the Colorado Territorial Fair. On the run into Denver, I began to hear mining stories—mostly good ones with little said about the failures. Silver was more attractive than gold because it was easier to find and averaged much higher per ton than was the case where gold was the only content in the ore.[1] The exhibits at the fair were very attractive, particularly a refined gold brick marked worth $40,000. All this created a strong desire to learn something about mining. As above stated, I got the benefit of mostly good stories with the hard ones left out.

On one of our trips west in the latter part of February 1871, we had on board our train a company of men who were on a mining expedition headed for the far-distant Little Colorado River[2] in Arizona. One of the party, Mr. Cole, claimed to know of a very promising placer proposition which he had found the year before while acting as scout in the government services. He claimed to have seen several small nuggets when lying down to drink at a running stream. That sounded good to a tenderfoot, and I was fool enough to quit my railroad job which paid $125 per month to enlist in their wild goose chase, putting up a $200 fee to do so.

I joined the party March 5, at Kit Carson where they lay in camp awaiting the arrival of the balance of the men. Our company, styled the Arizona Mining Company, originated in Chicago, Illinois. A group from Topeka, Kansas, joined us at Kit Carson. After paying my fee, I was furnished a Winchester rifle, a Remington revolver, a cartridge belt and ammunition, a long Bowie knife, and a knife and pistol holster. With all that on and with the razor left behind, I certainly felt like a genuine frontiersman.

We held a meeting on March 8 and elected Mr. Robbin captain, John E. Comerford assistant, and Mr. Cole as guide.[3] Going into a supposedly unexplored country, we laid in provisions to last for months. Transportation was secured by the company buying two large, new, overland freight wagons. No stock of any kind suitable for teams was to be had at Kit Carson. Captain Robbin hired a Mexican freighter with ox teams to take our loaded wagons over to the Arkansas River, some fifty miles south, where there were large cattle ranches and a chance to outfit with oxen.

On the morning of March 9, the freighter hooked up five yoke of oxen to the larger of our wagons and two yoke to the smaller. Our luggage and supplies formed a full load for the wagons; us twenty-eight men with our fierce armory buckled on followed afoot.

The Big Sandy, a stream usually dry but well known in Eastern Colorado, passes Carson about half-a-mile to the south. As the stream bed runs westerly and our road southwest, we had this to cross very soon after leaving the town. The bottom of this stream bed was very sandy, and two hundred feet or more across. As a matter of course, we stuck in it.[4] The usual amount of persuasion was offered the cattle by their Mexican drivers with their long blacksnake whips (lashes ten feet long with buckskin crackers), but a vociferous amount of cussing and hollering failed to induce the oxen to draw our wagons to the other side. Captain Robbin dis-

ships incidental to an overland trip of this kind had now begun to be fully realized. It required an effort on our part to always keep good natured. Sometimes we failed. One snowy morning, while breakfast was being prepared, H. J. Hutchinson[9] went into the tent and made some remark to Captain E. Comerford which riled his Irish temper. Comerford grabbed his six-shooter and ran at Hutchinson who came flying out of that tent much quicker than he went in. Needless to say, they were not intimate friends for some time afterward.

By March 18, the snow was about gone and the roads passable. We broke camp and got on the way, this time with our own outfit complete. The roads were not as good as we expected, however, and we made only twelve miles.

The following day, my twenty-sixth birthday, we pulled out of camp about 7:00 A.M. The cattle were only in middling condition due to the absence of grass at this place. On account of lack of fresh beef for over two weeks, we had grown exceedingly tired of dry salt bacon and thus did not feel much better than our cattle. As we were now getting out of the settlements, it was decided that it would be our own fault if we went any longer without fresh beef. Cattle were plentiful on the ranges along the road now. About 3:00 o'clock in the afternoon we sighted a bunch, and Joe Liebre tried his new rifle on a yearling. In a very short time the quarters were on the wagons, and we were moving forward as though nothing had happened. Fresh beef for supper that evening was quite toothsome, notwithstanding the manner in which it was obtained.

For the next few days we traveled through good cattle ranch country. High, round, haycock-shaped hills stood alone here and there, many of them covered to their summit with good grazing and a thin stand of scruboak and cedar. On the 21st we reached what appeared to be a divide of the drainage of the country, and camped on a good stream of water. The next day's march brought us into the foothills of the Raton Mountains.[10]

On March 23, after going about fourteen miles, we turned into camp. The cattle had been well fed with corn in the evening, and about 9:00 o'clock they took a notion to stampede, causing the guard much trouble. One of the men got lost in the brush but was soon found.

We did ten miles the following day which brought us to the eastern end of the Raton Mountains. Our line of march now took us through the mountains. Quite picturesque scenery was visible to the eye. Piles of curious rock on level ground seemed to have been so placed by some great convolution of the earth, as they had the appearance of having once been very hot.[11]

We now came to Emery's ranch[12] some 150 miles south of Kit Carson. The ranch had a little store and a few adobe houses inhabited by Mexicans and Indians, doubtless the employees of the ranch. This being Saturday, we found a good camping place four miles west of the ranch and concluded to rest through Sunday. Having already become accustomed to the frontiersman's manner of spending the Sabbath, we made no exception of this one. Nothing religious was done, and we spent the day washing up our soiled clothes and cleaning guns and pistols.

We hooked up the cattle and got an early start on Monday. After ascending quite a steep place in the mountains, we had before us a long, level, alkali bottom. About noon we passed a mountain which had a large crater in the center. It had undoubtedly once been a volcano. Toward evening we passed another.[13] We were disappointed in not finding water as expected, and had to carry what we needed for supper a distance of over two miles.

After dinner the next day, Sam Green[14] and I climbed to a high point from which we had one of the most beautiful views imaginable. We could see at least forty miles either way. The general surface was a little rolling, but looking east and south we could see, within ten miles of us, four round mountains which had evidently once been volcanos. There was a great amount of volcanic matter, burnt rock, etc., to substantiate the fact. On the north, the Raton Mountains presented a beautiful sight. On the west we could look over several small pine forests, some small knolls and the Rockies in the distance. In the southwest, from the foot of the heights on which we stood to a distance of some fifty miles, a valley was visible through which ran our road to Fort Union.

The next morning opened up beautiful—sky clear and sun shining. All went well until noon when we were about to stop for dinner at a beautiful spring. A cold, black cloud was fast approaching from the northwest, and soon we were in one of the most severe, cold and disagreeable equinoctial snow storms that I have ever witnessed. It came so fast and the wind was so strong that stopping for dinner was out of the question. To let the cattle loose would mean never to find them again. On we went, driven by such a terrific wind that both our teams and ourselves made twice our usual time. By five o'clock men and cattle were exhausted, and we had to stop with the storm raging.

There was no wood here except some logs hauled to establish a ranch. We pressed a couple of those into service and got something to eat as best we could. The cattle were turned loose that night without any guard. The next thing to do was make down a bed. It so happened that there was a stratified limestone quarry nearby. I built a little windbreaker of stone and spread my blankets. You can imagine my efforts getting into them and taking in as little snow as possible for a bedfellow. It was still coming down as hard as ever.

By morning the storm had passed, but our discomforts were still with us and not a hoof was in sight. However, we succeeded in getting some hot coffee and a bite of breakfast and got all our cattle together by noon. We made ten miles which brought us to the ruins of an old ranch on the Red River said to have once been one of Kit Carson's headquarters.[15] It was now used as a sheep ranch. It was still cold, and I made my bed down for the night in the sheep pen behind a stone wall.

Next morning we crossed the river. These western rivers are often seriously affected with quicksand which is dangerous. One sinks very fast in it, and in but a moment you can't pull yourself loose. A heavy ox train happened to be passing, and Captain Robbin paid them a dollar to put us over.

We reached Chicken Spring,[16] a little Mexican village eleven miles northeast of Fort Union, by evening. Here we saw the usual one-story adobe houses. Tilling the soil was carried out on a small scale with each one farming a little patch of an acre or two. There were no fences, although there was plenty of pine timber on the mountains within two miles. Their farm wagon was a kind of two-wheeled ox cart, and their plow was a curiosity.[17] They all had cattle but no hogs and few chickens.

Our next stop was Fort Union,[18] then one of the government's most prominent western outposts. This place, 250 miles from any railroad, was like an oasis in the desert. Outside of the government buildings there was a large store, well filled with first class goods, a butcher shop and a barber shop. Remaining here overnight, we awakened in the morning to find ourselves surrounded by a guard of thirty men from the fort. We soon found the object being to see if there were any deserters among us from Fort Lyon. Finding none, the guard was removed. We left there about 7:00 A.M., passing W. B. Tipton's store and Gregg's Tavern,[19] and camping five miles east of the latter.

Las Vegas,[20] some ten miles farther south, was our next point of interest. It had about 1,500 inhabitants at that time. This was a typical Mexican settlement, truly Spanish in every respect, with buildings and corral fences made of adobe. The adobe is a brick made of common mud mixed with some straw for reinforcement purposes. Usual dimensions are eight inches by sixteen inches and four inches thick. It is never burned—simply sun dried and laid in mud for mortar. Their bake ovens resembled an ancient straw beehive and also were made of mud.

We rented one of the corrals here and camped in it for two days. We bought four thousand pounds of flour, and our cook, Enoch Warrington,[21] tried his hand at baking a supply of bread to last the outfit for a couple of days, having what we thought was an honest to goodness oven to do it in. The next morning was Easter Sunday, and for breakfast we had some of the new bread. Never, since that day, have I seen such bread. Like government hardtack, it had to be broken with a hammer to get it into a tin cup for softening before we could chew it. As already indicated, we had a two-day supply on hand. Good humor among the boys was a scarce article while that bread held out.

Our next move brought us to Anton Chico,[22] another Mexican settlement of about five hundred people. This was on quite a stream of water, being near the headwaters of the Rio Pecos. After leaving here we began to ascend the Spanish Mountains up a long grade and over a rough road. At the top we found it quite disagreeable on account of the high wind. We traveled along this high ground until night and camped without any water. Early next morning we pulled out in search of water, but found none until 6:00 P.M. when we struck a little spring, or mud hole, which scarcely supplied our wants for the night. At this time we pressed into service a stray ox, yoking him in with an extra which we had with us. We were now on another cattle range, and Joe Liebre, the man who figured in the first beef venture, tried his hand again. In short order we had the hind quarters of another yearling in our wagon.

Our course now lay through what is called the Cañon Blanco, and a forty-five mile drive without water stared us in the face.[23] In order to get the cattle through, we were compelled to travel much at night. We laid over in camp until 4:00 P.M. The evening was calm and nice to travel, and we made eight miles, passing through Cañon Blanco of the Spanish Mountains. We turned into camp about ten o'clock to await the rising moon, resuming our journey at 2:30 A.M., still in Cañon Blanco which is about fifteen miles long. When we stopped for breakfast, John Coleman[24] shot a deer.

After two days and nights we reached water with man and beast exhausted almost beyond endurance. Through all of this we had a miserable, strong head wind to contend with.

After coming this far, keeping cool and good natured became a trial instead of a pleasure. Some indications of dishonesty and wastefulness had made their appearance. Ten of us, dissatisfied with the management, made application for a division of the outfit so we could go it alone. The captain and his party, being the majority, refused at that time, stating the inconveniences and disadvantages this would cause. There was much excitement in camp, however, and that evening they concluded they might as well let us go, seeing we were determined to go anyhow.

The following day, with Sam Green and myself representing our side and Stone and Campbell[25] representing the opposition, we made a levy on all things and divided equally among twenty-eight men.[26] We fell heir to the smaller of the two wagons and three yoke of oxen. All settled, they went on to Albuquerque while we remained behind baking bread and rearranging our own outfit generally.

We reached Albuquerque[27] the following day. The town at that time was the rankest kind of little Mexican adobe affair on the east bank of the Rio Grande. Here we rented quarters, cared for our cattle, and remained two days. As we were on this trip to reach new placer mines a long distance from any railroad transportation, we had to look out for what mining tools we were going to need when it was possible to get them. This town, though not a mining town, happened to have a small stock of placer mining pans at one of the stores, and we availed ourselves of what we thought we needed. I also bought a pair of rubber hip boots, paying seven dollars for them. Thus supplied, we were now ready for the mines.

We took an early start and crossed the Rio Grande on April 22, getting through the river sand about noon and laying over till evening. After having a rest, on we went, making short drives and resting often on account of our cattle being much run down by hard drives.

We passed Sheep's Springs and stopped three miles west of there to graze our cattle. We laid our scruples aside and pressed into service two good black steers that were running loose nearby, driving our exhausted ones as extras.

We reached El Rito[28] about 10:00 P.M. If ever I appreciated the light of a candle shining through the window of a

Mexican home, it was on that cold, windy night. We had stopped for a little supper about sundown so could stand it until morning with nothing more to eat. We succeeded in getting inside a corral and made our beds down behind a high wall. Getting out of there in the morning, we made about two miles and stopped for breakfast. All were blue and discouraged to the extent that several of the boys talked of drawing out. However, we tried it again and got a little more distance behind us. The team, notwithstanding all we had done, was badly given out, and we could hardly go at all. Just then a Mexican brought up a yoke of oxen, offering to trade but wanting twenty-five dollars to boot. This well nigh exhausted our pocketbooks, but we scraped it up. The fresh cattle made it go quite some better, and all took fresh courage.

We passed through Laguna,[29] an Indian town built on a high cliff of rocks, and camped one mile west of there for the night. In the morning we yoked up and passed Cubero[30] where we found an old Mexican prospector who offered to take us into the Sierra Blanca Mountains by a much shorter route than was possible with teams. The party with the larger wagon was also nearby at this time. In a joint conference it was decided to adopt this plan, and the prospector was hired as a guide.

Burros for pack animals were plenty and cheap. We managed to secure enough to outfit us. The larger party stored their teams at Cubero, putting their oxen in a pasture on a ranch. We went with ours to McCarty's ranch[31] several miles west of town. There were now eleven in our party. It required some time to adjust pack saddles and arrange the supplies that it was necessary to take, but finally it was accomplished.

The meeting place of the two parties was at the old Indian town of Acoma.[32] Nine of the boys started out, but

Sam Green and I decided to remain behind a few hours to see if we could capture an old horse that was running loose and seemed to have no owner. It took us the whole forenoon, but we met with success, and he certainly proved a big help, as will be shown later on. We finally overtook our party only to find they were way off their course, having tried to reach Acoma by directions, with no trail to follow. We put them on the right track, or at least we thought we did, and on we went, following the trail till moonlight but finding no water and no town. Waterman, being a good walker, followed the trail four miles farther and found water. He returned with a full canteen which was divided among us. When we reached the water, we learned from a ranchman who lived there that we were about twelve miles west of our destination. He put us on the right trail, and finally, after having wandered over some twenty-five miles or more to find a place only ten miles off, we did succeed in getting there about 9:00 P.M. The other party was on hand awaiting us.

We were now going into Indian country and the bigger party meant more security. Our first march to the next water was sixty-five miles and would take us thirty-six hours. With that ahead, it was thought best to rest up and start late in the day.

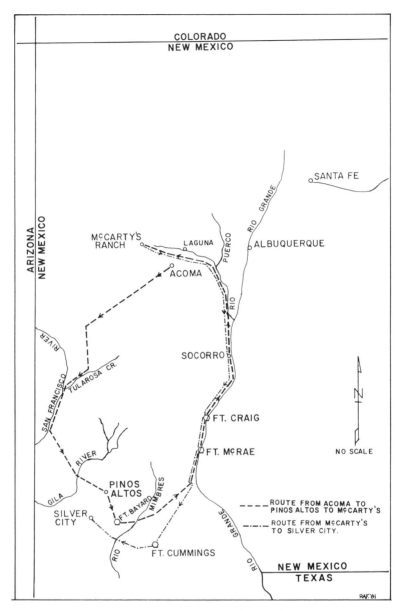

Route from Acoma to Silver City

3   A Worn-out Lot of Prospectors

Our course was now southwest to penetrate a country nearly two hundred miles square in which we would find no settlements by either whites or Spaniards. It was occupied only by deer, bear, wild turkey, and hostile Apache Indians.

We left Acoma about 3:00 P.M., camped for the night by the side of a lake, and pulled out early the next morning. Ahead of us was a drive of sixty-five miles to the next water. To get through, with the water supply we could carry, it was necessary to do much traveling at night. It was a hard drive, with both man and beast suffering some, but our guide always made things come out about as he said they would.

Around noon the following day we reached a nice little creek of running water. Oh, but it was a welcome sight. Sam Green and I, with our old horse, were among the first to reach it. Others, not so fortunate, had given out as much as five miles back on the trail. I filled up all the canteens I could get hold of, strapped them on the horse and went back to help the last of them in.

That afternoon, while traveling along through considerable timber, our guide saw a hawk in a big pine tree. He sneaked up and fired at it, scaring up a fine black bear who happened to be nearby in the bush. Times were lively for a few minutes as the rifles we had packed all this distance came into play, and Mr. Bear soon keeled over. We had bear steak for supper, and it was fine. Our camp that evening was noted for being the site of an Indian fight some four years before in which our guide's father and twenty others were killed.

The next day while marching along, we saw a flock of wild turkeys. Of course the boys went for them, and after a chase of half an hour they succeeded in getting three fine ones. We also saw two bears, but they got away. We camped that night in a cañon in the Sierra Blanca Mountains, laying over next morning to bake bread, while Baker, Davis, and Benardo went hunting. They got a deer which we picked up after having gone about five miles on our afternoon march.

We followed the little stream which proved to be a branch of a larger stream called Rio Bonito; this in the Sierra Blanca Mountains.[1] We reached the main stream and for three and a half days were in a cañon, crossing this little, clear, sparkling water from twelve to fourteen times a day. There was no trail except that made by bears. We had to fight our way through a thick growth of underbrush, scratching face and hands. Every little while a burro would rub his pack off against some tree or low, crooked limb and have to be repacked. We also saw some fine silver ledges, at least predicted so by our old miners. We were still in the cañon and camped on the same stream.

About the middle of the third day, we struck out on the bluffs and camped about two miles from the stream. As our guide didn't know where he was going any more than we did, our prospector, Benardo, took over. We now changed our course from west to south, marched about ten miles, and camped at the forks of the same and another stream.

We pulled out next morning in a southwest direction, marching up one mountain and down another, usually finding running water in the cañons and timber on the mountains. We struck a good trail[2] and on the second day this brought us to the head of a rather wide valley; no timber here, but in the distance a row of green cottonwood trees. We headed for this, following a small stream that ran south and emptied into the Gila River.

The next day we reached the river, and after following it about two miles our guide requested us to halt until he examined the ruins of an old fort. He found an old whiskey barrel-head with the shipping address still plainly visible. It read, "Fort West."[3] That showed him we were a long way off our destination. While at the river I washed a shirt, drawers, and myself all over.

We now turned back over the same trail we had come in on and kept this up for almost two days. Then turning northwest, we camped for the night on the first water met. This happened to be quite a meadow patch with good grass. As Caleb, one of our younger burro pack animals, was badly worn out, we left him here. In case we never came that way again, he would be free to run wild.

The next day our route was over a long, hilly trail. During the day, we saw a herd of sixteen black-tail deer, but did not get any of them. That night we had to camp in the hills without water. The boys were beginning to be discouraged on account of the hard marching and grub getting short.

Morning finally came, clear and bright, and about nine o'clock we met a party of thirty-two men coming from the river that we were headed for. These were the first people seen since leaving Acoma. From them we learned it was seven miles to the Frisco River, and that they were out after Indians who had been raiding in and around Silver City, the town they were from.[4] The Indians succeeded in reaching their reservation before this party could overtake them and were thus safe from attack.[5]

We reached the river in about three hours and found quite a respectable mountain stream for dry Arizona. Our course was now downstream, and we followed it for about nine miles. Getting lost and being forced to cover a good many miles three times was running us short of provisions. With no money to buy supplies and no place at which they could be secured, this situation was naturally very discouraging. Our guide now informed us that another day's march down the river and he would be able to show placer ground. Owing to our low provision stage, it was decided to encamp and send a detail of four of our most experienced men with him to give him a chance to prove his statement. Green and I loaned our old horse, and the others loaned their best animals. The next evening they returned, bringing with them three or four small nuggets about the size of wheat grains. This looked to us, then a lot of greenhorns, like a good prospect although a long way from the Little Colorado River.

Before we could go any further hunting mines, however, we had to hunt something to eat. Deciding to go to Pinos Altos, about six day's travel, for supplies, we now retraced our steps over the same trail we came in on. At the meadow patch where we left our burro, Caleb, we found him somewhat recovered and took him along. Camping there for the night, we saw smoke in the mountains to the southwest. There were no settlements in this wild place, so we knew it must be Indians. That meant a sharp lookout during the night, and I had a turn on guard from 11:00 P.M. to 2:00 A.M. Not being molested, we were not there the next night, and at the end of four days were back on the Gila River at or near where we first struck it and found our bearings.

We had already learned that Pinos Altos was on Bear Creek and the mouth of said creek was east of us. As these streams were our only guide, we naturally followed them, no matter how hard the going might be. Distance to the town from the mouth of the creek, we were told, was about thirty-five miles. By this time, we had almost nothing to eat. Here is the menu: bread made of flour and salt with nothing to make it light and spongy, tea, and gravy as we still had a little lard. Before reaching the town even this was cut down as both lard and salt gave out.

There was plenty of underbrush to fight our way through with worn out pack animals, but pulling off packs frequently was only part of our trouble. At one point we came to a precipice all of ten or twelve feet to the top and so steep it was almost impossible for a burro or horse to climb up. Two, three, and sometimes four attempts had to be made before reaching the top. We were in a box cañon and there was no going around to avoid this.

On the third day we reached the outpost of the town, where we found the cabins of two old California miners some two miles down the creek. They were the real thing. One, named J. K. Houston, had whiskers nearly a foot long; the other, a Mr. Thomas,[6] also had a heavy beard.

After a supper of bread and water, several of us walked in to see the town.[7] This was an old gold camp with both vein mines and some placer. It was situated right on the Continental Divide. Rain falling on part of it drained to the Atlantic and the other to the Pacific. The altitude here was seven thousand feet above sea level. With pine timber plentiful, the town was built of pine logs. There were two stores, a hotel, and an old quartz mill. Gulch mining was still carried on, but only paid about two dollars per day, and the place was overrun with strapped miners.

Entering a town as we entered this one, however, something to satisfy the inner man was a good deal more interesting than scenery and location. Several of our party, who still had a little change in their pockets, went to the hotel and had a square meal. The rest of us dug up the last coin and made up a purse to get a little sugar, coffee, salt and bacon for some more supper and a breakfast. That took my last half-dollar. For the next day's dinner we had to reach Fort Bayard[8] where fellows in our fix could draw rations enough to help them to the next post.

From here to Fort Bayard the distance was nine miles. We arrived there about 10 A.M. and made our starving condition known to the proper authorities. The distance to the next post, Fort Cummings,[9] was forty miles. This was considered two day's travel, entitling us to two day's rations, and this amount they donated. It consisted of hardtack, a little sugar, coffee, salt pork bacon, and a couple of pounds of pink beans. We made short work in putting some of this where it did the most good. While doing so, we found the soldiers here were quite interested in the Remington revolvers we had hanging to our belts and were willing to pay fifteen dollars apiece for them. As a result, nearly all of us sold that part of our armor, and we invested most of it in provisions. This put us in somewhat better shape for the time being, but it was no stake to go mining on.

We still had our team and some mining tools and other supplies at McCarty's ranch, almost four hundred miles away. Our party decided to get back to our wagon, dispose of it as best we could in that out-of-the-way country, and divide the proceeds. From then on it would be each one for himself and go where he pleased. The Robbin party concluded to return to the Frisco River.

The route via Fort Cummings was quite circuitous, and our desire was to reach the Rio Grande by the shortest cut possible. That meant trails over the mountains provided we could find them and then keep on them. This we decided to try, and our course from Fort Bayard was due east.

The first day out we stopped for dinner at the famous Santa Rita copper mine.[10] Famous now, yes, but at that time, May 1871, it was abandoned because labor was scarce and it was hundreds of miles to the outside world from all directions and over eight hundred miles to a railroad or tidewater. It was discovered somewhere around 1802 or 1803 and was used by its Mexican owners as a sort of Siberia for banished prisoners. Some of the cells were still visible at the time of our passing, also the iron rings to which they were chained at night.

After dinner we traveled about nine miles and camped for the night at a beautiful little reservoir formed by nature. This was in solid rock about eight feet long, six feet wide and eighteen inches deep.

Our next point of interest was the Rio Mimbres.[11] This was found to be a permanent, live, freshwater stream sufficient to produce from fifteen to twenty horsepower if properly harnessed. From here we tried to find the trail that would lead us across the Black Range and to the Rio Grande. During the day we made three attempts and finally camped on the river for the night. There were several ranches nearby, and one of the ranchers kindly volunteered to set us right in the morning. We went south six miles then turned east, finding the trail very rough.[12] This took us right into the Black Range which runs north and south and parallels the Rio Grande. While putting us on the right trail, our guide had the good fortune to shoot a deer. That, with our supplies, put us in pretty good shape for the next few days.

On the second night, while camping in a cañon by a small pool of water, our supper fire got the best of us to the extent that we set the mountains on fire. At that time there was no one living in them and so no protest. It would be a very different proposition should such a thing be allowed to occur this day and age. There are now mining towns, cattle ranches, and homes on every stream and valley.

After two more days of hard traveling, we reached the Rio Grande near the town of Las Palomas.[13] Our course was now north. On the west bank of this stream there were Spanish or Mexican settlements as early as the first settlements in the eastern state of Virginia. We had the benefit of this civilization for the rest of the trip to our wagon.

We passed Fort McRae,[14] which was located on the opposite side of the river. It was then occupied by U.S. troops to protect settlers from the Indians.

After passing several small towns, we reached Fort Craig.[15] Here officers and men were very hospitable, furnishing us a house to camp in (first time I had slept under a roof for many weeks), a corral for our stock and, on request, seven day's rations. While here we learned they were going to smelt some silver ore the following day. As this was something new to us, three besides myself remained to witness the smelting process while our main party went on. The ore was said to come from the Magdalena mines[16] west of the town of Socorro. We remained here until 2:30 P.M., then three of us set out to overtake our comrades while the fourth man, Ed Uli, concluded to enlist and stay there.

Four miles north of Fort Craig we passed through San Marcial,[17] a town of note. This was the neatest town we had yet seen in the territory. At 9:00 P.M., after a hard tramp of twenty-five miles, we found our party in camp.

The following day we passed through (Luis) Lopez, Socorro, Parida, and Lemitar, all situated in the garden spot of this river, and spent the night at Polvadera.[18] We could get vegetables and eggs while in this valley. Another day and we came to where our course must bear to the northwest up the valley of the Rio Puerco, a tributary of the Rio Grande only when it rains, which meant a thirty mile jaunt to the next water. Here we got off on the wrong road and lost a whole day. By a hard march next day, we found water in a hole dug in the river bottom. This helped us to eat.

Thirty miles more brought us to a little town where we passed the night. In the morning we found our burros corraled, with a penalty demand of five dollars for getting into someone's corn field. Investigation finally resulted in a settlement of ninety-five cents. No doubt it was a put-up job as they could show no damage done. This was at San Jose.[19]

By noon the following day we passed El Rito, some twenty-five miles farther on. I never knew what the word "tired" meant until we got into this abominable piece of country—twenty-five to thirty and forty miles from one habitation to the next. No white man, no matter how low, would stay in such a place. Alkali, cacti, desert scrubbrush, and sand; and this was in the month of June when one hundred degrees Fahrenheit is common.

We reached Cubero after another hard day of nearly thirty miles; from here to McCarty's was nine miles. This we made that night, arriving at 11 P.M., and you may rest assured there never was a worse worn-out lot of prospectors, if we were entitled to that name.

Our next move was to find a purchaser for our teams. This hung on for two weeks before we found one. As a matter of fact, plenty of impatience was manifested during this time, but we really got what was most needed, a good rest. At last a Mr. Provinger[20] of Blue Water made us an offer of $250 for our wagon and cattle, and a merchant at Cubero took our mining tools off our hands. That turned us loose.

As the team was to be taken to Cubero, we availed ourselves of this opportunity to get to town and outfit ourselves there. A Mr. Barth[21] was good enough to let us occupy a room free. He bought all our tools, cooking utensils and surplus supplies. At the end of three days each of us had found a pack animal for himself and was ready to go—but where? No one was fully decided. Some wanted to go to Camp Thomas, some to the Socorro silver mines, one to Santa Fe, and I didn't know which way to go.

Mining, so far as we could learn, seemed to be dull everywhere. This had a very discouraging effect on newcomers, but I was still not ready to give up the idea without giving mining a trial. Silver mining seemed the most attractive and was new in the southwest, but very successful in Nevada. We had heard the prospects at Silver City highly spoken of while at Pinos Altos and Fort Bayard, where we were within about eight miles of the place. The placer prospect on the Frisco River still had some drawing power, and as our only hope of success lay in finding something rich sticking out of the ground, the most likely place so far known was Silver City. I decided that would be my destination, and the rest concluded to follow to the same place. This meant right back over the route we had just come in on.

We spent the Fourth of July on the bank of the Rio Grande. Here I traded burros with a Mexican, giving him an old shirt valued at four dollars, and two pounds of coffee to boot, I getting quite a better pack animal.

The advantage of traveling with burros was that we could go where there were roads or no roads, in mountains or plains, and travel much faster than with cattle. However, days and days on foot with blankets and all you have to eat loaded on

a burro— edibles minus any vegetables whatever, had resulted in one of our party growing black on his limbs. It was
simply scurvy from too much salt pork and beans.

Continuing our journey, in due time we arrived at Las
Palomas. There, instead of the rough trail we had come out
on, we decided to stay with the wagon road via Fort Cummings, Rio Mimbres, and Fort Bayard to Silver City.[22]

4   Rat Hole Clinkers

We arrived at Silver City July 20, 1871, and camped on a creek of running water.[1] Nearby a garden was being culti- vated and young heads of cabbage were on hand. I lost no time in buying one and soon had it in my camp pot. Wait until it was well done? Oh no! I began picking at it when only half done simply for something different from baking powder bread, beans, and fat salt pork.

As newcomers were always welcome, we soon had callers. First came a visit from an elderly gentleman named "Adobe" Johnson.[2] He said, "I have an empty store building uptown that you are welcome to camp in. You are liable to get soaked by a cloud burst 'most any time now here on the creek." The offer was accepted at once, and we were soon under a good roof. This was some improvement after four months with the sky for a roof and your bed in a different place ev- ery night.

The next neighborly act was by Hughy Flynn,[3] who showed us some vacant lots to be had by simply building a cabin and moving in. I had now come to an agreement with Con- rad Shoemaker[4] on the cabin proposition, he also being a Pennsylvanian. As we had no money to buy materials, it was only possible to build because there were unused adobes abandoned by someone, and we could get slabs from a sawmill nearby. The cabin, built of adobes on a stone foundation, had a six-light window and a door in the front, and a four-light window in the back. Dimensions of ten feet by twelve feet left little room for beds and a table. To get around this we adopted the bunk idea, one above the other, with the table hung on the wall and dropped down when not in use. Stuffed coffee sacks substituted for mattresses.

A very short time after we were thus settled, the Indians made a raid on the town. My burro, being in fairly good shape for roasts, left with them; getting my permission was dispensed with. The sawmill needed a trusty man to herd the work oxen. Our youngest party member accepted the job. At the end of three weeks, the Indians saw an easy way to get a good horse and saddle, and put a bullet through his chest.[5]

As I had arrived at this place with no money and with no jobs in sight, I was compelled to seek help. The stores were very accommodating, but such favors must not be abused. I wrote to my late conductor on the Kansas Pacific Railroad and begged the loan of fifty dollars. In due time, I received a notice to call for a registered letter. I had to go to Pinos Altos to get it as Silver City had not yet risen to the dignity of having a post office.[6] The letter was from Mr. Hotchkiss granting my request.

I have said that silver mining was already highly successful in Nevada, and I will now tell what that had to do with bringing Silver City into existence. The mines on the great Comstock vein at Virginia City, Nevada, had a geologist or mining engineer by the name of J. Ross Browne. Mr. Browne, having business in New York, concluded to go by the southern route via El Paso, Tucson, San Diego, and San Francisco. This was by overland stage; there were no railroads here in those days. Driving along near what is now Lordsburg, New

Mexico, he saw a very prominent ledge outcropping which extended for a long distance over a hill on the south side of the road. It was not near enough for examination at the time, and he could only look as the stage passed along. On arriving at San Francisco, he reported the prospect of a second Comstock down in New Mexico. That resulted in an expedition being dispatched at once to locate it.[7]

The news soon reached the old gold mining camp of Pinos Altos. Immediately, they went to see the new discovery and said, "If that's silver ore, we have plenty near home." As soon as they could get to it, they plastered Legal Tender Hill with locations.[8] Legal Tender Hill lies just west of a nice little valley in which was a living spring of good water. On this flat piece of ground stood Silver City. It was about fourteen months old when I arrived.

Silver City is only about a hundred miles from the placer prospect we found on the Frisco River, and we still had that in mind. However, parties from here who knew of the prospect discouraged our going there now and advised us to look for high grade silver ore. Having again referred to the Frisco placer, I want to add that the next year, 1872, the Clifton copper mines were located only six miles from where our men got the gold.[9] These copper mines have been worked successfully ever since that time, now over fifty years, and have yielded millions. The placer we found was equipped with a hydraulic plant about 1883 or 1884 and failed.[10] There was not enough gold to pay, so it was lucky we didn't get to try it by the early-day methods.

By the time we arrived at Silver City, many residents had mining claims and a number had considerable ore showing good values in silver. As everybody needed money, the next thing to do was to get some of the ore into bullion. Some of the Mexican people had gained experience working with small furnaces in Mexico. As such furnaces could be built out of material then on the ground, namely rock and adobes, about a dozen such ventures were tried. They were in all parts of the town. The only one who ever produced any bullion was Mr. Carrasco, who had the right kind of ore and understood the business, having been successful in Chihuahua, Mexico. His success at smelting was largely responsible for giving this section of the country a favorable reputation. [11]

As there was no work to be had, I spent my time tramping over the hills looking for an outcrop of high grade ore. Most of the old party I came here with was loafing about doing nothing; among them were Mr. Robbin, our late captain, and Mr. Cole, the author of the Little Colorado River story. One day these two called on me and requested the loan of my Winchester rifle, saying they were going to the Burro Mountains on a hunting trip. These mountains, eighteen miles west of town, were well-stocked with blacktail deer. It was common to go hunting there, and I let Cole have my gun. Four or five days afterward, "Adobe" Johnson arrived in town from Las Cruces and stepped up to my cabin, handing me my gun. Surprised beyond description, I said, "Where in the world did you get that gun?"

"I took it from Cole and Robbin at Fort Cummings," he replied. "Found they were leaving the country and had borrowed your gun. Seeing you would never cast eyes on it again, I made them give it up."

That was the end of my experience with Mr. Cole. He was a hunchback in physical makeup, and not any better as regards truth and veracity. As already intimated, I am writing this long and many years after it occurred and know the

Little Colorado River has long since been settled up with ranches and towns and no placer ground worthy of the name has been reported.

Lee Campbell, another member of our party, about twenty-three years old, thought he was shrewd enough to live by the poker route (gambling). One night he got into a dispute over a game that was settled with six-shooters, and we followed him to his grave.

My prospecting in the vicinity of Silver City resulted in the discovery of a two-foot-wide vein of fifteen to twenty-ounce silver ore. This I located and named "Juniata" after my home county.[12] I sunk a shaft, hoping that the ore would improve as depth was attained, but at twenty feet the ore still showed no improvement in grade or value. Something better had to be found to produce any pay for the miner, hence more prospecting.

On this same district was an immense vein of what we now call quartzite, with a green stain of iron all through it. At that time nobody knew what that green stain was. I was lucky in getting a fifteen-hundred foot location on this vein.[13] It cropped for more than a mile and was from twenty to thirty feet wide. One young man in our party, Frank Whitmer, showed the same determination that I did to find something that would pay. I offered him a half interest, provided he would take hold and help sink a shaft. He gladly accepted.

First we had an average sample assayed; it showed a silver value of thirty ounces to the ton. Considering this encouraging, we moved on the ground, built a little shelter under a tree, and started a shaft. At about ten feet in depth, we put up a windlass to do our hoisting. Thus far it had been picking ground, but now one corner began to get hard—so much so that a shot was necessary. We proceeded to drill, using the old double-handed way where one holds the drill and the other strikes. Attaining a hole about fourteen inches deep, we proceeded to load. Fuse was not as reliable then as it became later, and black powder was the only explosive we knew. Frank went up and lowered the loading material to me. I cut my fuse a reasonable length to permit easy lighting; three or four inches above the top of the hole was the custom in a case like that. To give myself time to get out, I whittled shavings and placed them so the fire would not reach the fuse for a few moments. After touching a match to them, I was hoisted up.

The natural thing now was to wait and see the fuse spit then get away. It evidently did that while I was being pulled up, but neither of us heard the sound, if any was made, and we saw no sign that it was going. Both of us put our hands on the windlass roller and were looking for the spit when BANG went the shot. I was knocked down and out, but I soon came to enough to call Frank. Receiving no answer, I called again without trying to get up; still no answer. By this time I had recovered a little so I raised my head to look on my left where Frank had stood before the blast. Horror! There he lay on his back over a pile of what we were saving as ore. One eye was a mass of blood and the other was tight closed. I carried him to our cabin and stretched him out on the bed. He was unconscious and soon drew his last breath.

Using a new sheet of tin for a mirror, I looked at my own face. My left eye was only an immense clot of blood. Offering a prayer for Frank, I picked up my gun and started over the hills for Silver City.

The first man I met on arriving in town was H. H. White-hill,[14] sheriff of our county. Seeing my face all bloody, he grabbed me by the arm and said, "For God sake, what has happened?" On hearing my story he led me to our town doctor, M. H. Casson,[15] who washed my face and patched me up. I was then taken to my town cabin and put to bed. Whitehill secured a team and wagon, and brought in Frank's body. They told me they extracted a rock out of his eye almost the size of a hen egg. I had worn a black felt hat. On examining it I found a hole in the rim, on each side of my head, big enough to stick my thumb through. If my head had been one inch either way, I too would have long since been under the sod. It is easy to see that inexperience was the cause. My left eye healed up, but it left a mark in the eyebrow and the sight was injured.

This accident happened November 17, 1872.[16] In addition to this, the vein we were working on never has produced an ounce of silver for anybody. The button, if the assayer got one, came out of the lead flux he used and the silver out of somebody else's rock. This could happen if he did not prove his flux to be sure it was clean.[17] We did not know this then and were badly fooled.

Soon after I recovered, M. W. Bremen[18] offered a contract to Dan Dugan[19] and me to sink a twenty-foot shaft on his Republican claim, located on the hill just west of town and near my cabin. The conditions were as follows: he was to furnish us with provisions, powder, fuse, and tools; we were to have double wages (eight dollars per day) if we found pay ore.

The first twenty feet showed no ore. Not discouraged, Bremen gave us another twenty feet. The shaft was located on a porphyry and lime contact with two-thirds of the shaft in porphyry. At thirty-eight feet a shot in the lime disclosed a hole about six inches in diameter, extending back into the lime almost two feet. I reached into this hole and pulled out what I thought was clinkers, supposing the hole was caused by heat. Dugan, a man of forty or more, had no more idea than I that the hole meant anything. Two more feet and our contract was completed. We reported no ore—consequently received no wages.

By this time, several attempts had been made to produce silver bullion by amalgamation, and some success had been attained. However, it was soon found that this process was applicable only to certain ores.[20] An ore carrying galena pyrite of either iron, copper, zinc, or other base metals, could only be treated successfully by heat. That meant a smelter, and even this was still in the experimental stage.

A friend and neighbor of mine, David Winterburn,[21] had an old friend in Chicago named R. C. Anderson. Mr. Anderson was a physician by profession, but he also had promotional ability.[22] Winterburn said, "Doc Anderson is organizing a smelting company and will be here with a smelter within a couple of months. He proposes to sample your claims. If they show payable values, he will buy them and issue you stock in his company, thus making you a partner in both the mine and the reduction plant."[23]

This looked good to me, and I was anxious to pass the test. In due time the company and machinery arrived, and the mine examinations began. I knew my Juniata vein by itself would not pass. To help my chances, I went down into the Bremen shaft where I had worked a short time before, reached into the "rat hole", as we called it, and pulled out a piece or two of what I was calling clinker ore. I mashed it up along with Juniata rock and sent it in. It assayed thirty-six ounces of silver. I passed the test and received as pretty a bunch of stock certificates as you would care to look at, with a par value of $36,000. "Greenie" that I was, this gave me the first inkling of the value of the stuff in the rat hole. It also gave me standing with the company, and they put me to work.

It was soon quite evident that a lot of flux material must

be found before any worthwhile smelting could be done. Fire clay that would stand intense heat was needed; also iron, flourspar and lead ore. All this meant delay.[24] As money was running short, I found it necessary to look for something more promising. I decided to take a chance with Dave Winterburn and Robert Floorman.[25] The latter had made a little mining sale in Colorado before coming to Silver City. Having some ready money, he agreed to finance the proposition. Winterburn and I were to do the work.

We located a promising lead silver vein in porphyry formation over near the now famous Chino copper mine.[26] Here we built a cabin where Winterburn and I spent the winter. Floorman, having a family in Silver City, came and went. As it was only fourteen miles, he could easily do that.

Two fellow prospectors, John Magruder and James Fresh, had a claim nearby on what is now the Chino property.[27] As Magruder had a little money from his mother, they concluded to try their hand at smelting copper. They had a good showing of ten to fifteen percent green carbonate ore which was easily handled, and they were successful in producing copper bars. Our cabin was only a quarter of a mile above the little Santa Rita Creek which passed through both camps. I was frequently at their camp and knew they had also found some rather promising silver ore about seven miles east of their present operations.[28]

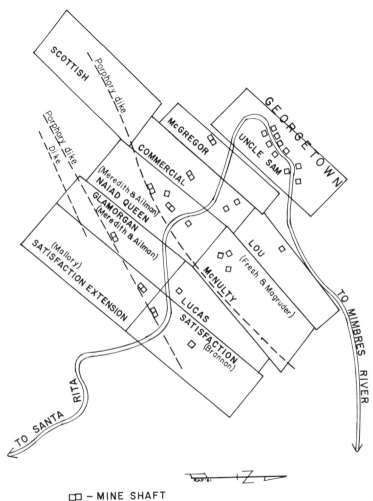

SCOTTISH

Porphory dike

Porphory dike Dike

GEORGETOWN

McGREGOR

COMMERCIAL

UNCLE SAM

(Meredith & Ailman)
NAIAD QUEEN

GLAMORGAN
(Meredith & Ailman)

LOU
(Fresh & Magruder)

(Mallory)
SATISFACTION EXTENSION

McNULTY

LUCAS

SATISFACTION
(Brannon)

TO MIMBRES RIVER

TO SANTA RITA

RAF'81

☐☐ – MINE SHAFT

Georgetown Mining Claims

45

5 Beyond the Day's Pay Brigade

Springtime came along, and we decided that our lead prospect at Santa Rita was not any too promising. Fresh and Magruder were putting some men to work on their newly discovered silver property. I asked them for a job and lost no time in moving over there. Our new camp was known as Georgetown, called after a town of the same name in Colorado.[1]

Mining work was still all the old double-hand way, and I was assigned to go with a short, heavy-set man named Hartford M. Meredith.[2] He was quite bald, with a heavy beard, and had a mild disposition. We soon became warm friends. He was from the Julian district of San Diego County, California. He had ridden a sturdy pony alone across Indian-infested Arizona over the old Butterfield stage route. He left a fairly good gold claim at Julian in charge of a partner who had power of attorney to handle it in case a buyer was found.

We were not together many days before we began, in our primitive way, to geologize the formation and predict possibilities of the extension of the ore bodies we had been set to work on. The ore was found in a limestone formation, capped by a heavy black slate.[3] The ore was very high in silver—clear carbonate of lead which often showed value as high as fifty cents per pound and was easily treated by a Mexican adobe smelter which was nearby.

The company ground extended less than two hundred feet west of our shaft. The adjacent ground had a location notice and a ten foot shaft, but it showed no sign of ore, nor was there an outcrop in sight anywhere on the claim. The new United States mining law, then only two years old, required sufficient work to show ore and to determine its course.[4] Previous work had failed to do this.

Thinking we could beat wages, we took a lease on a piece of company ground near our former hole. This we tried for some two weeks, all the while discussing the possibilities of this extension. The company was running a tunnel toward the extension right along and taking out 150-ounce-per-ton milling ore. The lease streak was rich but small. My anxiety got the better of me, and I proposed to Meredith that I draw out of the lease and start a shaft on this extension. He agreed and decided to continue on the lease alone. The company work, our lease, and my proposed shaft were only two or three hundred feet from one to the other.

The parties interested in this extension, Byron Allen, William Mulvenon, and Thomas Roach, had wintered with Dave Winterburn and me over in the Santa Rita camp. I had a location over there on which I had found nothing but iron. About the time I moved away, Allen, in walking over my claim, broke a piece of rock and found it full of lead carbonate. A little digging showed a nice little vein six or eight inches wide. Now they too had come to Georgetown, and were the locators on this ground Meredith and I had our eyes on. They said that I could have this ground if I would give them my claim over in the lead camp. I, knowing nothing of Allen's find, readily agreed. Thus my starting shaft was neither a claim jump nor a fight. They thought they had quite a bit the best of it.

Meredith picked a raw Dutchman, just over, to work with

me. He said he could talk five languages—German, Irish, Spanish, English, and American. I could hardly understand his way of handling either of the latter two, but we managed to get along. After going down about twenty-five feet, the layers of slate began to get rather thick (four, five, and six inches) and very black. The road passed near our shaft. At this stage, Magruder went by on his way to Silver City. On arriving there, he remarked to people who knew us both, "I passed Ailman's shaft today. It looked like he was hunting coal. I'm sorry to see him fooling his time away on such a showing. He will never find anything there."

We knew it would be forty or fifty feet through the slate before we could reach the limestone, and expected no ore in the slate. At fifty-two feet I struck the lime, but no ore. A porphyry dyke intruded the lime formation and it cropped on the surface. On the contact of this lime and porphyry dyke existed the ore capped by the slate. I had worked in Fresh and Magruder's tunnel and knew this. Not knowing which way that dyke might pitch, we kept twenty feet away so as not to run into it before reaching the lime. A drift was now started straight for the dyke, and it proved just as far in to it as we had gone from it on the surface, thus showing that the dyke was almost perpendicular.

To be sure we were safe, we decided to have a legal decision on the mining law before any new strike was announced. This made it necessary that I should be the first one to know if any ore was found. I had the advantage of my five language Dutchman, George, who was working for $1.50 per day. At nineteen feet, I was on top working the windlass and now watching every bucket closely. Heretofore, it had been all smooth, slippery slate. Now there were several pieces of a salt and pepper permeated rock which showed me that George had hit the dyke. I immediately called him up and I went down. Working as hard as I could, I sent up bucket after bucket, breaking everything with the sledge. Finally a little bump stuck out in the lime. I whacked it loose with the hammer, picked it up and examined it closely with the candle. "That's not lime," I told myself. "I believe that's ore."

As the shaft bottom was pretty dark, I had George hoist me up, went behind a bush and examined it in the daylight. It looked mighty good. I went on down to where Meredith was working on his lease, called him up and said, "The dog is dead. Look at this."

"My God, that looks good!" was his answer.

The company's general manager, Elija Weeks,[5] was within hailing distance and friendly to us. We called him over and let him in on the secret. Extending hearty congratulations, he arranged right there that I should shut down and in the morning go to work for him. Meanwhile, he circulated the story that I was out of money and must recuperate my finances before doing further work.

All the while, George was standing at our windlass awaiting my return. He was the first to learn that tomorrow there would be nothing doing. The windlass was removed and also the ladder so that no one could descend. Next day I was working as above indicated.

Saturday finally arrived and Meredith went to Silver City. Using fictitious names, he presented our case to one of the best lawyers and received the opinion that "the party doing the work to discover and determine the strike, or course of his vein, could hold against all ten-foot location holes or shafts showing nothing." Thus assured of our being safely within the law, George was reinstated, the windlass was reassembled, and work resumed. The report was now allowed to get out that we had struck it. The ore I had shown, assayed seven thousand ounces of silver per ton. The strike report was given out November 9, 1874. The name given our mine, on perfection of location, was the "Naiad Queen."[6]

Up to 1873, the double standard of both gold and silver had prevailed and silver stood at $1.29 per fine ounce. During 1870 and 1871, the Franco Prussian War settlement demanded and collected one billion dollars in gold from France. That put Germany in excellent shape financially, and resulted in their agitating for the adoption of the single standard of gold. The United States, debating the same question in 1873, passed a law virtually demonitizing silver, and President Grant signed it. This was the law later designated as the "crime of '73." The effect was that we were never able to get $1.29 per fine ounce for our silver.[7]

Silver mining was a tremendously important industry in both Mexico and the United States. In order to stabilize silver values, our Congress passed a law authorizing the U.S. Treasurer to go into the market and purchase two million fine-ounces of silver per month for coinage purposes. This later was increased to four million and resulted in keeping the price of silver bullion close to, and sometimes a few cents above, $1.00 per ounce. This continued during our career with the Naiad Queen.[8]

Although there was no reduction plant nearer than Silver City, we had no trouble in producing free-milling ore that would yield over one hundred ounces of silver per ton. This soon put us beyond the day's pay brigade. Our neighbors, Magruder and Fresh, heretofore referred to as "the company," now began the erection of a five-stamp mill driven by water power. It was located on the Rio Mimbres, three miles east of the camp.[9] With the ores being of the free amalgamating variety—mostly chlorides and horn silver—this put us on the map as a successful mining camp.

Having so far lived in a small log cabin, our first urgent need was a building in which we could house our help and have some accommodations for ourselves. We manufactured adobes and erected a building. This made us fairly comfortable, and it was now easy to have a sum of ore treated at the Magruder mill when in need of money.

It was now well along in the summer of 1875, and I had been away from home for nearly six years. Thinking myself now financially able, a trip east to visit my parents was about the right thing. I arranged for my partner, Mr. Meredith, to take charge during my absence. We were working five or six men, all of them on good ore, and this was to go on while I was away.

I started about the first of November. These were stage coach days, with the nearest railroad at Pueblo, Colorado, five hundred miles due north. However, the first hundred miles of the route was east to the Rio Grande and the town of Las Cruces. From there we went north over the *Jornada del Muerto* and via Albuquerque, Santa Fe and Las Vegas. The veterans who once enjoyed a week or more of this kind of travel, day and night, are like the veterans of the Civil War—badly thinned out.

At Santa Fe there came aboard a ministerial looking gentleman with a high plug hat. Stage coaches have quite a rocking capacity, sending you fore and aft on short notice, depending on the depth of the gully the wheels struck. Along in the night, and halfway asleep, we hit a good one, our heads awful near the roof. Down came the plug hat almost to his shoulders. His remarks I will not repeat.

I finally reached Pueblo. Oh, but that train looked good to me, an old railroad man who had not seen a train for six years. The next stop was at Denver where I had left my trunk and best suit of clothes with my former conductor, Samuel Hotchkiss. I also handed him the fifty dollars he so kindly loaned me years before.

I spent a day or two in Denver noting the advance of railroads since my disappearance from that city. Then, with an entire new outfit of clothing and a through ticket to Philadelphia, I once more boarded a Kansas Pacific train. This time it was over the old run and on to Kansas City, St. Louis, and Pittsburgh, frequently changing trains. Through transportation then was not developed to the accommodations available today. My home being a hundred and fifty miles west of my ticket destination, a stop off had to be arranged. I left the train at Mifflin, our county seat, hired a livery carriage and was driven out home where I received a hearty welcome from my family.

During the Civil War, men in the service had little or no chance to shave, and wearing a beard was all the go. This prevailed for years afterward, especially on the frontier, and I was no exception. Now past thirty, I had not shaved for three or four years—certainly some change.

I was the first of the grown-up set in our neighborhood to make a break and venture away out into the wild Indian country of New Mexico and Arizona. Now a safe return elected me to a heavy siege of helping to dispose of their Christmas gobblers. More than once, I felt like asking for the ax and a chance to tackle the wood pile and thus get some much needed exercise. Holding their spellbound attention for hours by relating my experiences and what I had seen afforded me great pleasure.

About March first, my brother Jerome[10] was ready to return to Princeton College in New Jersey. I went with him to see the sights. After a day or two I returned to Philadelphia and took in the Centennial Fair grounds, then in the course of construction. Here for the first time I saw a Japanese pulling a plane instead of pushing it. I could not remain for the opening two months later. I spent a few more days at home, then purchased a ticket to the western terminus of the A.T. & S.F. Railroad at Pueblo. From there to my destination was again by stagecoach.

On my arrival at Georgetown, it was into a pair of overalls and to work. The six men on when I left were still at it and had advanced the tunnel work about a hundred feet, all the way in good ore, and a pile of thirty or forty tons was on the dump. C. P. Crawford,[11] then running the Tennessee Mill[12] at Silver City and doing custom work, sampled and purchased our ore. This gave us a capital of twenty thousand dollars to work on after paying off our men, one of whom had let his wages run till we owed him thirteen hundred dollars.

Development up to this time caused James A. Lucas[13] to think he could make a custom mill pay. With a ditch taking the water just as it left the Magruder mill, he had a little over a twenty-foot fall in about half a mile. He built a penstock and installed a turbine. His capacity was about one and a half tons per day. He soon found that he could not do enough work to pay, having no ore of his own. On top of this, his turbine was too large for the water he had, which made his power very irregular. However, his ditch and mill site were desirable, and we had no trouble in buying him out.[14] We removed his turbine, installed a twenty-foot overshot water wheel, and we had ten horsepower, always reliable. We installed a new five-stamp battery with the requisite number of amalgamating pans and a Frue vanner.[15]

This now gave us a number one, five-stamp, amalgamating silver mill, and put us in shape to handle our own ores.[16] But first, we had some adverse experiences. Our head mill superintendent, John Spillar,[17] had some previous milling experience, but your last seldom fits the new place. Our first brick was nearly half lead, and the second not much better. However, a little experimenting with salt, concentrated lye, and several other chemicals constituted the right combination, and our third brick of 1,000 ounces assayed 990 fine (1,000 being pure). We were now in shape to run night and day and needed a reliable man to take charge of the night shift. To supply this need, I sent to Pennsylvania for my brother Sam.[18]

Reports that Indians were out on the warpath, or that a new strike had been made, were nothing to get excited about as they occurred frequently. The country was only about five years old from a silver mining standpoint. High assays were now reported from a new find over south of what is now Lordsburg. Although we had plenty to do at home, Meredith decided he must see what might possibly develop. Our new Studebaker half-spring wagon and a pair of young, fast mules were just the rig for such a trip. He took with him Fitch, one of my best men out of the mine. Their route lay via Santa Rita, Silver City, then eight or ten miles south of where Lordsburg is now, in unsettled country.

All went well and the morning came to start home. In packing, they thoughtlessly put their guns in first and blankets and other bedding on top. The weather was fine, the roads good, and a lively gait was kept up. This was a treeless area with visibility good for long distances, but from some strange freak of nature a little grove of two or three acres of whip-like oaks, ten to twelve feet tall, sprang up and flourished. The road passed near this grove. Without any warning, BANG, BANG, BANG went a volley of rifles. Indians! The first thought was a lash of the whip to get away. BANG, BANG again, and both animals dropped. Neither man was hit, but they knew their turn would be next. Making a scramble for their guns, they got down on the opposite side of the wagon from where the shots were coming. Nearby happened to be a cañon with a fair sprinkling of greasewood bushes and banks high enough to afford some protection. They made for this.

The cañon proved to be quite lengthy. It was now a running fight, but don't get your head above the bank; dodge from one bush to another and peek for a shot. The redskins were careful to keep out of range, so there was little hope of hitting any of them, but it had the effect of keeping them from getting near enough to get shots at you. The attack, which began before noon, continued all afternoon. Toward evening Fitch was hit in the instep and disabled. Then Meredith was hit by a bullet which had flattened out on something else; it broke two ribs.

By this time it was getting too dark to take aim. Meredith, still able to move about and knowing the gullibility of the Indians, concluded to try a trick to scare them off so he could get out to get help. Building a row of boulders around Fitch's body for protection, he stood up and shouted with all the force his lungs would produce. It had the desired effect. The Indians made for their horses, left back where the fight began, and Meredith crossed the hills to the new camp and got help. A team went out and brought in Fitch.

In the morning they made a new start for home, this time getting safely by the grove. On arriving at Silver City, Meredith left Fitch in the care of a doctor and was able to continue on home. Imagine my surprise and dumbfoundedness when I saw a new team, new driver, and no Fitch. I said, "For God's sake, what has happened?" Then I heard the story here retold.[19] The new find they went to see never amounted to anything.

Meredith, in due time, fully recovered his health and took up his abode at the mill, boarding with our mill builder and his family who lived in one of our houses. We now settled down to our regular business of mining and milling—I the mining end, and he the milling. Almost a year had passed when Meredith came up to the mine one day and informed me that he and Minnie, the mill builder's daughter, were engaged. Owing to the great disparity in their ages—he was thirty-eight and she was fifteen—I was greatly surprised, to say the least. As long engagements were not in style on this frontier, in April 1878, I acted as best man at their wedding, thus cementing that family for the remainder of their lives.[20] The minister, in this instance, was our precinct justice of peace.

During the month of June, a new family consisting of husband, wife, and grown-up daughter passed through our camp. I soon found out they were from Kansas and were looking for a new location. They found several unoccupied adobe houses at the Santa Rita copper mine, seven miles east of us, and got permission to move into one of them.

I now had a Negro cook and was boarding seven or eight men. There was but one brand of condensed milk in existence at that time—Borden's sweetened—and we had not learned to use it. If we had cream for our coffee, we had to keep a cow, and this I was doing. Cows do not like confinement and will stray if a chance offers. Mine got the chance and away she went. I mounted my whim horse[21] and started out to find her.

This newly arrived Kansas family had brought two or three cows with them. It was only natural that one animal would hunt another for company. With this good excuse, I called and inquired. The conversation soon became quite agreeable as I had had quite an experience in Kansas several years before, and had also been over much of the route they had just passed over. Furthermore, the father, Ira E. Smith,[22] who was a carpenter by trade, had been here almost all of the year before in the employ of Robert Black,[23] a planing mill owner, builder, and contractor. Most likely Mr. Smith had helped get out the material that was in our overshot water wheel, as Black had the contract. With a pleasant invitation to call again, I returned home. We did not run the mine on Sunday, and it soon became common knowledge as to where I could be found on that day.

A term of the district court came along. About every other term almost the same set would be selected as jurymen. On this particular occasion our little town paper got hold of the list, and published it before the sheriff got around to serve us. With this advance information, we saw a chance to dodge without being called down for it. A so-called prospecting trip was hurriedly planned by five of us. Our destination was the headwaters of the Gila River, thirty miles north and equally as far from any other settlement. Here the river is formed by three respectful-sized creeks. Following the west or larger one up two or three miles, we came upon a fine specimen of an old Cliff Dweller's village situated, as was their custom, in a crevice where there was good protection afforded by a wide, overhead ledge of projecting rock.[24] In this case, from floor to roof was about eight or nine feet. The walls were of small, flat stones laid in common mud, with no door or window frames. The walls lacked twenty inches of connecting with the roof, to give the smoke a chance to escape. They had their fireplaces in the center of the apartments.

In searching for relics, the only thing we could find was corncobs, very small, four to five inches long, and only in thickness about like your largest finger. A fair sample of these

57

I took with me. This dwelling was about two hundred feet up a steep hill from the creek. We concluded that they selected such sites for protection. Needless to say, Miss Virginia got the corncobs, but Sheriff Whitehill failed to find Ailman anywhere near the Smith residence, as he fully expected to when he could not find him at his mines in Georgetown.

When the next season came around, another party from our town made a trip to these same ruins. Prowling around from one apartment to another and passing through a so-called door, they discovered a loose stone. On pulling it out, a cavity was disclosed in which lay a package. Curiosity excited, they investigated further and found that this was the last resting place of a young infant, apparently only a few days old. It was thoroughly dried up and weighed only a few ounces. The face was quite distinguishable, and there was a little tuft of hair still on the back of its head. Later it fell into the hands of a friend of mine who photographed it, making several pictures, one of which is within my reach as I write. The remains were sent to the Smithsonian Institution.[25]

Miss Smith had brought her favorite riding horse, a gray Indian pony, from her old Kansas home. We took frequent rides about the surrounding hills. During these rides, I learned much of the Smith family's past life and sorrows, decided Miss Virginia was the one I was looking for, and told her so. After a short deliberation on her part, the answer was in the affirmative. On July 28, 1878, eight days after her twenty-second birthday, we took the vows administered by her father, a Methodist minister.[26] As witnesses we had H. M. Meredith and wife, and my brother Sam.

In preparation for this event, we decided to close the boarding house as the town was nearby, and the men could easily find accommodations there. Thus Virginia found a big, empty house with no one but me to look out for. I paid off Saturday night as usual, nobody the wiser, and on Monday morning the men coming to work found a lady in charge. Here was the time for a honeymoon, but in our case it had to wait a while.

Some of our mining drifts were almost under the house and when shots would go off, the jar was very much felt. In following our main vein, we had left behind quite a promising indication heading off at right angles. This I now concluded to prospect, following it for some twenty feet. One day as I came in, the boys informed me that they were up against a perpendicular limestone wall; heretofore, it was slate. I said, "Raise up to where the lime goes flat again." This proved to be some seven or eight feet, and a shot in the lime was needed to see what it would show. This shot off, my main miner in the drift came hunting me up and asked for a sheet of canvas. I asked, "What's up? Is your partner all shot to pieces, and you want to gather him up?"

"No," he replied, "It's not quite that bad, but we have something I want to take care of."

On going to the house and asking my wife for a piece of canvas, she too got suspicious and wanted to know if something awful had happened. I said "No, the boys have struck something good."[27]

This upraise made it necessary to sink a new shaft, as it would be very inconvenient to mine this ore and put it on top via the tunnel. The location decided on proved to be only fifty feet from the kitchen door.

C. P. Crawford, our banker and merchant at Silver City, every now and again had visitors from back East—young men hunting their fortune out West. Not being able to employ them in his business, he would send them out to us with a letter of introduction and request that we give them something to do if possible. At this time we had two of them, Harry W. Elliott[28] and J. D. Pancake.[29]

Of course, they knew nothing of our kind of work. Elliott, who was six feet two inches tall, was no good below because we could not afford to run tunnels big enough to fit him. I taught him to sort ore, which would keep him on top. Pancake was introduced to a wheelbarrow and put below. In that day mucking was a much more cumbersome job than it is today. Mining cars and track now in use were not then invented. With us it was wheelbarrows, homemade and plenty stout, ironed in our own blacksmith shop. Pushing one of these was Pancake's job, and it took all the muscles he could raise.

It was a common custom for men to work several months, getting two or three hundred dollars saved up, then go prospecting, with the hopes of striking it rich. Harry Elliott and his partner tried one of these trips. With burros for pack animals, they went west, roaming over part of Arizona and returning via Stein's Pass where they found a small carbonate lead vein which they hoped would pay, but it didn't.[30] One evening after an absence of several months, who should stop at my door but them—shoes worn out and rawhide tied on with thongs to keep their feet off the ground, clothing all rags. The first salute was, "Harry, can you give us a job? You can see we need it." They were put back to work.

One day I rode down to the mill. On the way I passed two men afoot, carrying their blankets. I saluted them and inquired their destination. They said, "Georgetown." Further inquires disclosed that they were coal miners from Kansas. After telling them what my work was like, they said they would like a chance to show their hand. I directed them to my camp and put them to work. One was named Robert Forbes, and the other Harry Pye.[31] The latter carried with him an accordion. He was pretty good at grinding out music, and all enjoyed his evening's entertainment. They worked several months, and were all I could ask for as miners. The prospecting fever, always contagious when a little money had been accumulated, now bit them. Outfitting in the usual way, they headed east for what is known as the Black Range, lying parallel to the Rio Mimbres. Soon after getting into the mountains, they were met by the Indians, and Pye was killed. Forbes escaped and came back and worked awhile. Then he and Elliott tried it again in the same range. This time they were successful and made a handsome fortune out of silver ore.[32] Another set of my men made a trip through Arizona, Nevada, Utah, Colorado, and back to me again, asking for a job. That was the life of a miner in those days.

Just above the Naiad Queen was another porphyry dyke and lime contact. The strike, of course, was the same as ours; the ores were high grade, but in smaller bodies than with us. This was covered by two different owners. Bill Mallory, who was somewhat easy going, was on the west, and Stanton Brannin[33] was on the other side. Brannin was married and had quite a family. He also had plenty of temper, and oh, how he could use profane language. Brannin and Mallory soon got into a dispute over their boundary lines, with the result that the former took a rifle shot at the latter, hitting him in the foot.[34]

With this bad blood on, and us doing pretty well, we saw a chance to settle the matter by buying them out. Meredith first tackled Mallory and soon struck an agreement.[35] Meredith's father-in-law, Mr. Bunn, had a gold watch which he thought he could get a good price for by working it in on Bill as part payment. Bill happened to like the idea, and Bunn got a hundred dollars for a well-used watch.

We already had a half-interest in Brannin's end of this

property and were dickering for the other half. Our men, working on this ground, had opened up a fine pocket of soft sand carbonates. Just shoveling them into sacks, in two days we took out two thousand dollars worth. A blast here exposed a so-called "rat hole" in the lime, which I intended exploring later on.

Brannin was holding out for fifteen hundred dollars and Meredith was offering him twelve. Our recent strike excited talk in town. Three men who had some money shoved fifteen hundred dollars into Brannin's hand and became the owners of that half-interest, putting us in partners with them, which was anything but satisfactory. We now sold our half in that claim to them for two thousand dollars, and I carried their check to the bank.[36] They, now in full possession, explored my above referred to "rat hole" and soon were filling sacks with sand carbonates. This opened my eyes and taught me what those holes meant, learning also what freak of nature produced them in lime formation. The loss of that claim no doubt had much to do with our later being offered $160,000 for the Naiad Queen instead of the $180,000 we were asking. Meredith had tried to save three hundred dollars and lost twenty thousand.

Over a year had now passed since our marriage, and the stork had paid us a visit, resulting in giving us a young son named David Eugene Ailman. During the summer of 1879, the Apaches made their usual summer raids and called to see what they could steal in our neighborhood. My father-in-law's young mules were driven off, and my partner's fine saddle horse was taken out of a padlocked corral at the mill. The Indians used a wire rope to saw a section out of the adobe wall. Wire rope was new to them, but they soon found ways to make it serve them. A day or two later, along came General Crook, with a sizable detachment of mounted soldiers from Fort Bayard, looking for said band. Of course they never saw an Indian, and no one ever recovered their lost stock. Historians today write up General Crook as a great Indian fighter. This scouting trip did not differ from many others he made. [37]

Magruder and Fresh had now mined up to their end line. This was the boundary between their property and ours which cut off much of their ore supply, making it necessary for them to look elsewhere for something they could make pay. Leadville in Colorado, and Tombstone in Arizona, both yielded ores similar to Georgetown. Magruder, being something of a promoter, decided to try Leadville. [38] There he made the acquaintance of James D. Hague, [39] a noted mining engineer representing parties in New York City who were looking for something good to take hold of. The A.T. & S.F. railroad was building south from Pueblo, Colorado, heading for El Paso, Texas; the Southern Pacific, building east through Arizona, was also heading for El Paso and on to New Orleans. This being the situation, Magruder had no trouble in persuading Mr. Hague to visit Georgetown and look over his and our properties. [40]

We were employing about twenty men at the time and producing bullion right along. There were three or four three-hundred-pound bricks of fine silver stored in our kitchen at the mine. The reason for pouring such large bricks was to make it impossible for pack mules to carry them off in case of stage robbery. It would require two bricks to make a pack balance, and that would be a load beyond the capacity of any mule. We were down three hundred feet on the porphyry contact and had several showings of high grade ore. This contact was almost perpendicular while the other, between the lime and slate, was horizontal, also carrying the same grade of ore.

A week's examination of the mine and nearby formations brought a favorable report. We asked $180,000 for our holdings; Magruder, having the little end of it, asked $40,000. This resulted in our putting a deed in escrow with the First National Bank of New York City. It lay there almost a month before a wire arrived offering us $160,000. I was the first to suggest our acceptance. Meredith soon agreed and replied by wire saying that we accepted. Three or four more weeks passed, with us mining and milling just as though no deal was on. At last another wire—option exercised and the money in the bank to our credit. That stopped operations for our account, but not the work. Everything went on as usual, but a new set of books was opened.[41]

In cleaning up, we produced two more of those large bricks. Considering it risky to ship by stage, we hired an unsuspected mule team with a driver well known to us. His name was Ben St. Cyr.[42] We posted him as to the load resting on the bottom of his wagon bed with several old blankets carelessly thrown over the cargo. Meredith and I, both mounted on good horses and heavily armed, followed four or five hundred yards in the rear, and it went through without anything happening. The bullion was dropped on the ground in front of C. P. Crawford's bank. From there it went to the assay office to determine its fineness and estimate its value. We got an additional credit at Crawford's bank of $43,000 and owed only $5,000. This transfer occurred April 1, 1880.

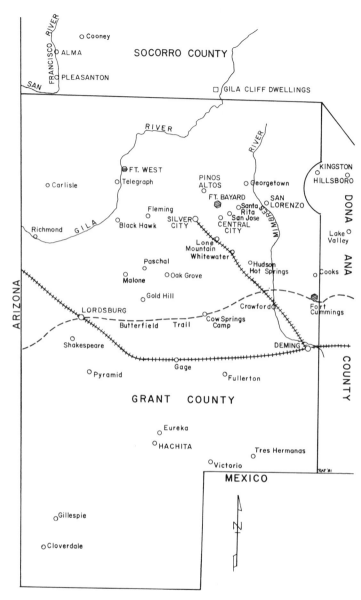

Grant County, New Mexico, 1885

66

6   Much Going and Coming

As before mentioned, the Santa Fe and Southern Pacific Railroads were making rapid progress by 1880. Their courses would soon effect a junction about forty-eight miles southeast of Silver City. At this point a new town was bound to spring up, giving this section transportation easily reached—a great improvement over what existed before.[1] The several Silver City merchandising firms had all prospered during the preceding years. Range for cattle was excellent, extensive, and just being stocked. Silver mining was at its height, with many mines producing, and also one copper camp seventy miles to the west. Silver City was headquarters for both shipping and banking.[2] That being the outlook, we decided to make our homes there and go into business.

One of the larger Silver City firms was owned by an elderly gentleman, Joseph Reynolds, who wished to retire. We looked him over and bought him out.[3] This put Meredith and Ailman in the business of merchandising. In the trade we acquired a sawmill in the Burro Mountains, eighteen miles west of town. Not caring to go into that line of business, we turned the mill over to Robert Black, building contractor, as part payment on two new residences, one for each family.

The new houses were to go up on a vacant block we bought from Isaac Stevens.[4] On this block three wells or holes had been dug, hoping to get water. All were over twenty feet deep, but showed no water. The road to Black's planing mill passed close by one of these holes which had no guard around it. One day soon after the ground became ours, an ox team came along with a young and partially broken in pair who concluded to try their luck at bucking to get away. Just as they were passing this hole, they succeeded in getting loose. Their first move was right over the hole, and down they went, one on top of the other. It took a block and tackle and a bit of engineering to get them out without injuring either one.

Our two houses, being virtually paid for in advance, came slow. It was more than a year before mine was ready to move into.[5] In the meantime, a rainy season passed and a respectable-sized flood rolled down over our lot. To keep this from happening, we built a two-foot stone wall along the west side of the block with a five-foot adobe wall on top of that, and filled up those holes; hence no more trouble. We established a line through the center of the plot giving each a half-block, and then tried our hand at finding water on said line so as to supply both houses. Going down near forty feet— more than half of that in solid granite—we got plenty of water, but it was awfully hard. To remedy that, I built a hundred-barrel cistern and piped all my roofs to it, passing through an improvised filter of sand and charcoal. I had splendid soft water—so much so that the doctors would use it for their sick patients.

The establishing of a new home was simply a side show in comparison with our store which occupied nearly all of our time. We carried close to a hundred thousand dollar stock, employing four to five clerks.[6] With all freight transportation from the end of both railroads still by ox or mule team, forwarding and commission firms kept abreast of the front terminals and accepted all our freight from the railroads, settled bills, and forwarded our goods to us. Browne, Manzanares & Company were our agents.[7] It was not uncommon for them to send us a statement showing us indebted to them in the sum of five thousand dollars. They never lost a cent on our account.

With this class of transportation, it was an easy matter to be out of certain lines before new supplies arrived. More than once was flour all gone, and we were patching up crackers and any other substitute that could be devised.

While the railroad front was at Socorro, I made a trip there on business. At the best hotel the flies were so thick on the table that you had to be on constant watch to see that none were on the bite on your fork. Never since have I met anything like it. The partitions between the rooms in that hotel lacked about two feet of connecting with the ceiling. Every word spoken in the next room was easily heard, and the conversation was sometimes rather spirited.

I have told about General Crook's way of hunting Indians who were out on depredating trips, and his success—or lack of it. Uncle Sam now decided to try a new deal; that was to hunt Indians with Indians. The latter had to be willing to engage in that kind of business, as it often proved to be brother hunting brother. However, it was tried, and met with better success than the former method.[8]

Eventually the Indian Scouts' time was up, and they were paid off. This being their nearest town, in they came wanting clothing. One would buy vests. Selecting one, he would put it on, choose a second, and put that on on top of the first; a third selection went the same route. Another wanted a hat, and the same process was followed to the extent of four. Now comes one wanting underwear—drawers and undershirts. He too started packing his purchases for trans-

69

portation in the above described fashion, and was only stopped when persuaded that his camp would be a more appropriate place for that move.[9]

We had a profitable trade wholesaling to merchants doing business in Chihuahua and Sonora, Mexico.[10] They would come in caravans of twenty-five, thirty, and forty pack mules. On arrival, their first move would be to see who would make them the best price on *manta* (unbleached muslin). Whoever caught them on that would get all their trade. I have carried their silver dollars to the office by the gallon. They also brought silver *planchas*—fine silver which they had produced in their small adobe smelters. These planchas had much the shape of an ordinary pancake from the breakfast table. This trade ended when the Southern Pacific Railroad reached El Paso, as they could then save much in the packing distance.

The Southern Pacific was now almost a hundred miles past the junction where the Santa Fe would connect, and the town of Deming had sprung up. During the first year of this railroad's operation, four men—I can't recall their names—concluded to pick up some easy money by holding up and robbing a passenger train. They selected Gage, the next station west of Deming, committing murder in carrying out their scheme. However, they soon were caught by our sheriff, H. H. Whitehill. This landed them in jail only a few blocks from our store.[11] One day, several weeks after the fellows had been locked up, word suddenly sprang around town that the train robbers had broken out of jail and were escaping. Mr. Jackson,[12] who was on the street with his delivery wagon, was one of the first to hear of it. He jerked the harness off his horse, an exceptionally fine animal, mounted him bareback and succeeded in keeping the robbers in sight until the sheriff's party came up, which they did within a few minutes. The robbers had grabbed several rifles in overpowering the guards. Many shots were exchanged, with the result that three of the robbers were killed. The fourth, badly wounded in the leg, managed to escape, but was captured two weeks later and sent to the pen for life.[13] One of our townsmen, Joe Lafferr, took too much risk and was killed in the fight.[14] My wife and I attended his funeral.

Some years earlier, a young man from New Orleans named James Cooney[15] had enlisted in the U.S. Army and was stationed at Fort Bayard. Eventually his time was up and on being mustered out, instead of going home he concluded to try his hand at prospecting. This resulted in his finding a valuable claim in the Mogollon Mountains. The ore was rich in copper, gold and silver. During his first year, he was killed by Indians while working on his claim alone in that isolated section.

A year later James Cooney's brother, Mike,[16] who had the reputation of Faro dealer, came out to look after his brother's mining claims. This resulted in his interesting Eastern capital in investing some sixty thousand dollars for development work. Included in this work was the completion of a five-stamp mill equipped with Frue vanners for concentrating the ore. Getting money out of that kind of ore was Greek to all at that time. The Easterners came out and looked the thing over. They came to the conclusion that it was a white elephant and would advance no more money. They posted a notice to the effect that Cooney could continue, but anyone working for him would have to look to him for their pay.[17] The name *Cooney* indicates his nationality—Irish—and his help was mostly the same. The capitalists now gone, Cooney called his men around him and explained the situation. "Boys, you see the fix this leaves me in. Now we have this mill. Will you stand by me for two weeks and let me see what we can do concentrating that ore?"

Their reply was, "B'Jaysus, we will."

At the end of the two weeks, Mike loaded up six tons of concentrates, and in due time drew up in front of our store. Meeting me, he said, "Ailman, I have a batch of concentrates on these teams. I wish you would unload them in your warehouse, sample and assay them, and see what you can loan me on them."

His request was granted, and the sampling showed they carried 150 ounces of silver, to say nothing of the copper, with no hint of gold so far. There being six tons, and silver worth close to a dollar per ounce, the lot was good for at least nine hundred dollars. We advanced him eight hundred dollars which put him in shape to continue. In about two weeks, he came in again with another six tons. Nearly all smelters were then on what was known as a lead base, and only one, the Argo[18] at Denver, Colorado, handled ore with a copper base. To them I shipped this ore. In about two weeks, we received a check for eighteen hundred dollars. This wiped out our loan and gave Mike credit of a thousand dollars. He was now able to produce a full twelve-ton shipment without our help, and again he received a check for $1,800 in return. The third shipment went over $2,000, the fourth $2,800, the fifth $3,600, the sixth over $4,000, the seventh over $6,000. There was now also gold in the ore, and the eighth shipment was worth $13,800. Within six months he had a balance to his credit on our books of over $40,000. Up to this time all drafts came as did the first, payable to Meredith and Ailman. Thus we handled his money direct from the smelter and know whereof we speak.

The Easterners now found their white elephant had changed color, and they came out for division. From then on, the smelter was ordered to remit to them, and thereafter we only got the payroll money at the end of each month, but the mine paid over $300,000 before it pinched out.[19]

We had their trade throughout the life of the operation, but not without occasional Indian trouble. Mountains are rather rugged and well-timbered in this area, with many points near the road suitable for Indians to hide. One of our shipments to Cooney consisted largely of flour. At a place known as Indian Point, the road ran close around the point of the mountain. Here a lot of large blocks of rock had fallen off the mountain, some on each side of the road. In the middle of that bunch, where the boulders were the thickest, was found the freight wagon, with flour sacks ripped open and contents scattered over the ground. The mules in the team had been driven off, and the driver lay beside the road with five or six bullet holes in his body. The Indians had waited until he was within a few steps of their hiding place. Nothing was ever recovered.

The Mimbres Mining Company, our Georgetown successors, made an arrangement with us to furnish them with currency to meet their monthly payroll.[20] They reimbursed us with a draft on their New York bank. On one occasion their demands were rather heavy, and they required $13,000 to meet them. We knew the risk involved in forwarding that amount by public transportation should it be known. At the same time, our Georgetown branch store[21] had requested a bill of goods. In the lot was a bolt of unbleached muslin. This was undone and the currency placed inside. Then it was repacked and loaded on an ordinary freight wagon and so delivered safely to the proper parties.

We had now been in the mercantile business for almost a year. Our new homes, though progressing slowly, were approaching completion, and it was necessary to buy new furniture, as what we had was unsuitable. In addition to this, we had had no honeymoon since our marriage, and my people had not met my wife. I decided now was the time for a trip east.

Although the railroads were coming, the Santa Fe was still three hundred miles away. We were still in the stage coach era and had to resort to that mode of travel to get out of the country. It took twenty-four hours to reach Las Cruces—no Pullman comfort in stage travel. Breakfast over, it was all aboard again for the journey across the *Jornada del Muerto*. This was once a ninety mile drive without water, but at the time of our trip, a well had been sunk midway of that distance and a stage station established. The name of this station was Martin's Well,[22] and it was where we landed about 2:00 A.M. the second night out. There were no accommodations for a coach load of passengers, but the driver was humane enough to offer me his bed for my wife and child. With a chance to lie down, we all piled on, not even removing wraps or top coat. The driver rolled up in his blanket on the dirt floor of the room.

We had ham and eggs, potatoes, baking powder bread, and black coffee for breakfast. It was sixteen miles from here to the end of the track, with our road frequently crossing the railroad grade. These were steep, sidling crossings, and to prevent danger of upsetting, we were invariably requested to get out and foot it to the other side. The train was waiting at the end of the track, and although only an old day coach, it was the most appreciated car we ever boarded.

Socorro was the established terminus at that time. The regular train schedule was such that we were again obliged to patronize the same hotel in which I had stopped before; accommodations had not improved. The next morning we had the pleasure of boarding a full-fledged passenger train with Pullman sleeper. From then on we could travel in comfort, reaching my old parental home without encountering events worthy of note. Suffice here to say that we had an overdose of roast turkey and entertainment. We took in Philadelphia, visited my wife's relatives in Oswego, New York, and were favored with an extreme cold snap with plenty of snow. We stopped over at St. Louis and bought the furniture for our new home.

On our return west, we found the Santa Fe Railroad had crossed the Rio Grande and proceeded westward to within forty miles of the proposed junction with the Southern Pacific at Deming. Again hitting the end of the track away after midnight, we had to leave a comfortable train for the cold and uncomfortable stage coach, with one consolation—this would be the last time. Hereafter, we would have the railroad all the way.

On arrival home, we found our house completed and ready for occupancy. In due time the furniture arrived by ox train. It was in good shape, with only one dining chair being damaged, and made our home most comfortable. The cultivation of a lawn and planting of trees soon followed. I also added a stable, a pair of fine grays and a new carriage that could be easily adjusted to carry four people. Soon after we were settled, a daughter arrived whom we named Theora Pearl.

As my wife was brought up a Methodist, and the only Protestant church in the place being of that denomination and nearby, we soon became members and regular attendants. Soon thereafter the Episcopalians formed an organization, and we shared our building with them until they finally grew strong enough to build one of their own.[23]

The country was still new, and the many business ventures being sought entailed much going and coming.[24] Soon after taking hold of Reynolds' store, I sent for my brother

Jerome, residing in Pennsylvania, to come to us and take the position of cashier and bookkeeper. This he accepted and held for a year when his health gave away to the extent that prospecting and roughing it seemed to be what he must adopt.[25] It fell to my lot to look for his successor.

I sent for a young man named John Smith, who was a neighbor at the old home and got his education along with Jerome.[26] He came on and served for about a year, then he requested a leave of absence of a month to go back to get married and bring out his wife. To this we agreed, and it presented an opportunity to have my father and mother pay us a visit as I long had hoped for. Both were still in good health, with their family all grown up and off for themselves. They were regular home bodies, never having traveled over a few miles on a railroad. I knew they would never undertake to make this trip of over two thousand miles alone, but with Smith and his young wife, whom they knew well, it would be easy. I supplied Smith with the assets and ordered him to bring them along for a visit.

One old neighbor, whom father had known since boyhood days, said, "Why, Mr. Ailman, a man of your age can't stand a trip like that."

Later on, aboard a fast through train and after their first night in a Pullman sleeper, with beds tucked away for the day and sitting comfortably in their seats, Father nudged Mother with his elbow and remarked, "A fellow who could not stand this couldn't stand anything."

With the railroad now completed to Deming, it was only a fifty mile stage ride to Silver City. Knowing of their arrival at the former place and the stage schedule, I had my handsome pair of grays hooked up to the carriage and with my wife drove out about twenty miles to meet the stage. I took off my party of four and landed them at my new home.

Theora Virginia Smith Ailman. (Ailman Scrapbook)

Harry Ailman (left) and his partner Henry Meredith. (Ailman Scrapbook)

Georgetown, New Mexico, 1878. (Ailman Scrapbook)

The Ailman home at the Naiad Queen mine, Georgetown,
New Mexico, 1878. (Ailman Scrapbook)

Store and mill of Fresh and Magruder (Mimbres Mining and Reduction Works) on the Mimbres River. (Courtesy John Harlan Collection, Silver City Museum)

The Gila Cliff Dwellings c. 1912. (Courtesy John Harlan
Collections, Silver City Museum)

Remains of the old Spanish fort at Santa Rita, built around
1804. The fort was in the form of a triangle, 150 feet to a side,
with round towers at each corner. (Ailman Scrapbook)

Mexican cart similar to the one Ailman saw in Mexican villages en route to the Silver City area. (Ailman Scrapbook)

Bullard Street at Broadway, Silver City, New Mexico, c. 1888.
The corner building at left is the Meredith and Ailman
building. (Courtesy John Harlan Collection, Silver City
Museum)

General mercantile store and private bank of Meredith and Ailman, 1882. (Courtesy Silver City Museum)

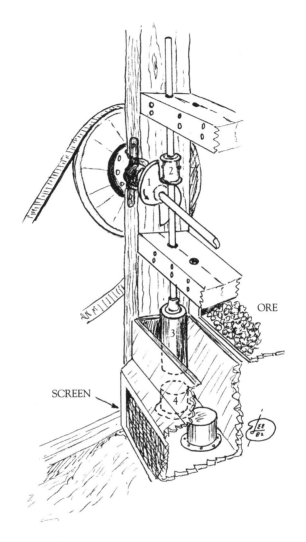

ORE

SCREEN

Cutaway view of stamp mill. Ore is fed in from the rear. Cam (1) lifts tappet (2), raising shaft and attached shoe. Tappet is released, allowing shoe to drop onto die (4), crushing ore. The mill was usually set up in batteries of five stamps which fell in sequence.

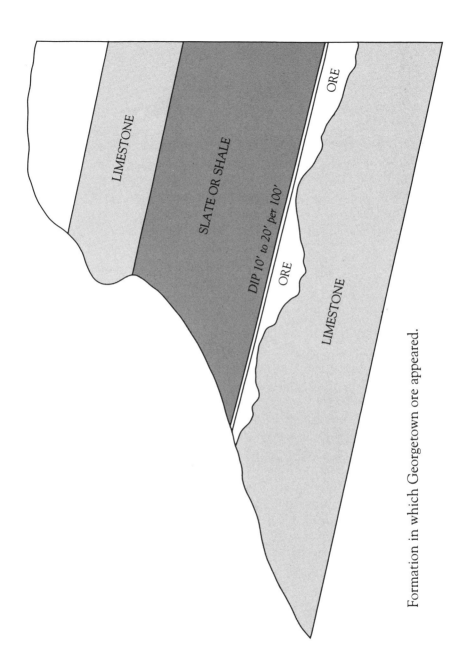

Formation in which Georgetown ore appeared.

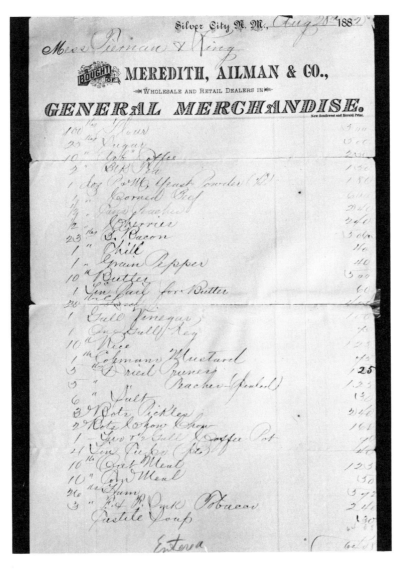

Bill of sale from the Meredith and Ailman mercantile store,
1882. (Courtesy John Harlan Collection, Silver City Museum)

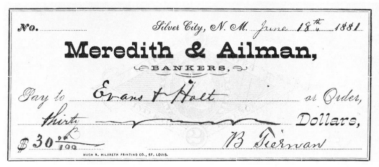

Meredith and Ailman Bank in Silver City after 1883. Ailman is on the left, Meredith is second from the right, and to the far right is Col. J. W. Carter, cashier for Meredith and Ailman and later for the Silver City National Bank. (Ailman Scrapbook)

Check from Meredith and Ailman Bank. (Courtesy John Harlan Collection, Silver City Museum)

Silver City National Bank, southwest corner of Bullard Street and Broadway, in late 1889. The building, unique among Silver City structures because of a cut stone facade on its east exposure, stood until 1922. (Courtesy John Harlan Collection, Silver City Museum)

The Ailman house (left) and the Meredith house on Broadway, Silver City, shortly after their completion in 1881. The building is now the Silver City Museum. (Ailman Scrapbook)

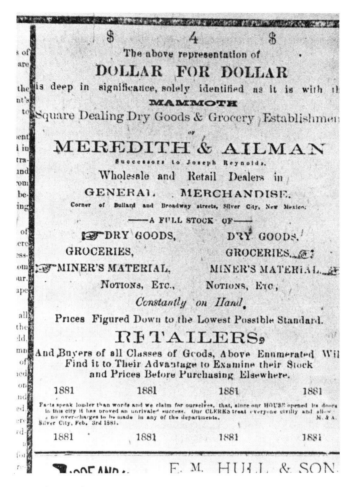

General merchandise advertisement for Meredith & Ailman.

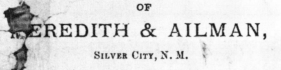

BANKING HOUSE

OF

EREDITH & AILMAN,

SILVER CITY, N. M.

CAPITAL - - - - $200,000.

Transacts a General Banking Business.

Foreign and Domestic Exchange Bought and Sold. Issue our own drafts on all parts of Europe. Collections made on all available points, and remittances made promptly on day of payment. This bank has superior facilities for transacting legitimate banking in all its branches. Highest rates paid for

GOLD AND SILVER BULLION.

CORRESPONDENTS:

New York—Chemical National Bank. Chicago—First National Bank. St. Louis—Laclede Bank.
New York—Kountz Bros. San Francisco—Wells, Fargo & Co.'s Bank.
Santa Fe—First National Bank. Las Vegas—First National Bank. Tucson—First National Bank.
Chihuahua City—McManus & Son.

Bank advertisement for Meredith & Ailman.

Father and Mother considered that the greatest event of their lives.

A few days after their arrival, we received a shipment of onions grown on a farm in the Rio Grande bottom. I knew they were much above anything Mother had ever seen, notwithstanding the fact that she was an exceptionally good gardener. I sent for her and Father to come and see the onions raised in a country where rains are few and far apart. After the surprise over the onions was over, Mother, seeing the scales nearby, suggested weighing to see how they were standing the trip. Father found himself near a keg of horseshoes and slipped several in his coat pocket. Of course, he surprised everyone with the gain he had made since leaving home.

During their stay I saw to it that they rode over the Naiad Queen silver mine where I was the discoverer. They also saw the famous Santa Rita property. Since their visit, it has produced millions in dividends and is still productive. One day we visited Pinos Altos where my father-in-law lived at the time of their visit. On the way we passed a cornfield from which part of the water flows west and eventually reaches the Pacific Ocean, and the other part flows east and into the Gulf of Mexico. Few cornfields have that record. The continental divide passes Silver City about six miles west; slope at that point is very gentle.

My parents remained with us about four months. February 1883 now well along, they felt it was time to get back to the old farm and look after things. Jerome wound up his affairs and went with them. Coming via the Pennsylvania Railroad and the Atchison, Topeka & Santa Fe, and returning via the Southern Pacific to St. Louis, gave them quite some view of the West and put them well above their old neighbors as globe trotters.

Among our customers was a prominent lawyer from St. Louis named Judge McComas,[27] who had a family of wife and three children. The two older were girls about nine and twelve, the youngest was a five year old boy named Charley. Mrs. McComas was a member of the Methodist Ladies Aid and quite friendly with my wife. At that time they had frequent meetings at the church, trying to teach a class of Chinese the English language.

Judge McComas, as a lawyer and prospector, had quite a clientele and was much away from home. I have seen him appear in court, just in from the hills with a month's growth of beard, to address a judge or jury, and oh, how the words flowed with no hesitancy as to what he would say next.

A strong mining company had a twenty-stamp silver mill over south of what is now Lordsburg. McComas was their attorney. Something needed his advice, and this made a trip to the property necessary. Thinking to make part of it a treat for his wife, he asked her to go along. Placing the two girls with neighbors, they took the young son, Charles, with them. Their vehicle was a buckboard with a pair of speedy young mules.

The first day out, they traveled thirty-five miles to a ranch in the Burro Mountains where they spent the night. The following day, only a few miles took them out of the mountains onto a vast level plain. Just before the road led onto this plain, only a few hundred yards out of the cañon, there was a thicket of some three acres of scrub oak, ten to twelve feet high and quite thick. The road led near this, but not through it. As they passed this spot, jogging along mule-trot fashion, BANG, BANG went a charge of rifles! Knowing what this meant, and hoping to escape, the whip came into play. More shots followed quickly and down went the mules and Judge McComas with them. That left Mrs. Mc-

Comas and the boy absolutely at the mercy of some fifteen or twenty wild Apache bucks. You can imagine the rest!

The news soon reached town, and a party went out and brought in the bodies. The boy, Charley, never was found, and for a long time the Indians would not tell what they had done with him. Finally some of them admitted that owing to his yelling and screaming, which he would not stop, he had been killed. [28]

7 An Unfortunate Turn of Events

The railroads had now reached their junction, and further need for overland freight teams was wiped out, except for the gap between that point and Silver City, a distance of forty-eight miles. Local agitation now began to grow for a branch line to make ours also a railroad town. It grew until it resulted in the incorporation of the Silver City, Deming, and Pacific Railroad.[1] I was elected treasurer, and at this time I was also holding the office of city treasurer.

The year 1881 had been favored by an exceptional good allowance of rain. Consequently there was a splendid grass crop, which meant that the herds were in fine shape. Mining, both silver and copper, was prosperous, having a very beneficial effect on both banking and merchandising. During the next two years our principal competition, C. P. Crawford, took hold of a gold proposition in Arizona called the Golden Rule mine, developed it to a depth of some three hundred feet, and installed a twenty-stamp reduction plant. The ores failed to yield anywhere near the bullion expected, decreasing in value as depth was attained.[2] This reduced his finances to the extent that one morning, somewhere in 1883, we were surprised with the information that the Crawford institution, and also the Grant County Bank, would not be open for business. That left us, the Meredith and Ailman Bank, alone in the field.[3]

As already indicated, we had built up quite a banking business in connection with our merchandising. In March 1883 we had a chance to close out the store and devote all our time to banking. Max Schutz[4] was the buyer and thus became our successor, paying us two hundred dollars per month rent for the store and warehouse. We owned the building and retained the north half for bank offices.

By this time the country had filled up with cattle, involving many heavy investments.[5] The years 1884, 1885, and 1886 were not up to normal rainfall. Feed demands by increasing herds on the range naturally produced cattle in poor condition. The price of silver was being kept up by the silver purchase law then in existence which required the government to buy four million ounces of fine silver per month for coinage purposes.[6]

These were the conditions in Grant County when one day we were called upon by a Mr. Raynolds,[7] president of the First National Bank of Las Vegas, New Mexico. During the conversation, he drew a check for $12,000 and requested that we place the same to his credit, stating that he might make an investment. In further interview, he suggested that it would be a good idea for us to establish another bank, and to make it National to keep out competition.[8] That looked like good advice, and after due consideration moves were made with that end in view.

It was necessary to have a board of five directors and $50,000 capital. John S. Swift,[9] a successful hardware merchant, was selected, and he advanced his share of the money. John Brockman,[10] a prominent cattle rancher, had to borrow his share, so we made him the loan of $15,000. Meredith and myself furnished the balance. David Goldman,[11] a

97

bright, well-educated young man, and a relative of Mrs. Meredith, was a director and cashier. The matter of organization proceeded by obtaining a charter, arranging for the issuance of National Bank currency, and securing the vacant bank building on the opposite corner, built by C. P. Crawford. Meredith and Ailman bought the building. All this done, the Silver City National Bank opened for business.[12]

C. H. Dane,[13] a former Wells Fargo express agent at Lordsburg, married into a wealthy family and succeeded in establishing a bank in Deming the same year. It also happened to be the year for the election of county officers. Some of Meredith's friends urged the use of his name for treasurer on the Democratic ticket, C. H. Dane being selected on the Republican side. Meredith, being much better known and considered more solid, won out.

Range conditions grew worse, and money was continually being drawn out. We requested Mr. Brockman to raise his $15,000 investment from some other source, as we needed our money. He finally reported that he could get it at the First National bank at Santa Fe, depositing his Silver City National Bank stock as security, provided Meredith and Ailman would endorse the note. This was unpleasant for us, but we needed the money. We accepted, and the $15,000 was placed in the Silver City National Bank to the credit of the Meredith and Ailman Bank. We would call for drafts as we needed the money.

During this same year, Mr. Dane succeeded in organizing a branch of his institution in Silver City, thus increasing outside competition. All was moving along apparently quiet, however. We had a balance of some $30,000 in cash in the Meredith and Ailman Bank and were feeling quite comfortable. Then, on the afternoon of December 6, 1887, we were informed that we might expect a run on our bank the following day as someone was circulating whispering reports to the effect that the Meredith and Ailman Bank had grown weak. This, of course, was an infamous lie, but convincing our depositors of this fact before opening time the following morning, or getting our available cash in our vaults, was impossible. We had valuable real estate which was all clear, much was due us on notes, and our standing in Bradstreet was rated A-1; but none of this could be turned into ready cash to meet a run the next day.[14]

There was but one step we could legally take, and that was to make an assignment for the benefit of our creditors.[15] A secret meeting was held in the director's room of the Silver City National Bank that evening. Present at that meeting were John Brockman, Hartford M. Meredith, David Goldman, Thomas Conway,[16] our attorney, and myself. After discussing the situation, the decision already stated was agreed upon.

The matter of preferred creditors arose. Meredith spoke up and said, "I want the county to be the first preferred creditor, and Max Schutz the second." Mr. Schutz was on an accommodation note he had signed for us, which was rediscounted in New York.

Brockman now arose, beckoned Meredith to a corner of the room, and begged to be put down as the third preferred creditor, stating that it would be impossible for him to take care of the Santa Fe note. Meredith turned to Conway and said, "Can we do that?"

Conway's answer was, "You can prefer anyone you want to." Those words were the sole cause of our assignment being annulled, or set aside, for they were absolutely unlawful, as we later found out to our sorrow.[17] Mr. Conway's bill for that service was the exact amount of the note he owed us—$1,000.

That laid us liable to attachments, and they came thick and fast on everything they could lay their hands on. H. W. Elliott, who had a deposit of $2,000 with us, was one of the first to come to trial.[18] The case was tried in Sierra County, and Brockman was called as one of the witnesses. On being questioned about the $15,000 loan, he swore that he had carried the money to pay off that loan (in currency in a hand grip) and delivered it to Mr. Meredith in person at the bank office. The reason Brockman was not immediately prosecuted for this perjury was that Meredith had left the country and gone to Snohomish, Washington.[19] The public was suspicious of that Brockman preference. I was the only one who knew the facts, and it was to our interests not to give them out at that time.

Our downfall naturally paved the way for Brockman to become president of the Silver City National Bank. With George David Goldman, our assignee, as the cashier, that put all our assets in the vault of that bank. Soon after this became a fact, it was reported that several of our largest and most solid notes were missing. The notes were finally paid, although it was never established as to who was responsible for their disappearance.

Things drifted along now for about a year, during which time the court ousted Goldman and appointed William A. Leonard,[20] a newspaper man and friend of mine, to succeed him as assignee. Brockman now gave it out that he was the owner of the Silver City National Bank building. That compelled me to take action. I called on Mr. Leonard and gave him the actual facts in the case. He then suggested that he and I meet with Judge McFie, and I repeat the facts before him. This resulted in Leonard bringing suit against Brockman to quit title, and winning.[21]

Brockman, now a bank president, was in a position to

become a mine promoter. Smelters had found a large deposit of hematite iron near the Santa Rita mine, a very desirable flux for their smelting operations. Brockman succeeded in getting an option on the property, and also in finding buyers, and made a handsome profit.[22] I had known of the deposit for years, but never had an opportunity to handle it. The demand came just as he fell into his advantageous position.

The men he succeeded in interesting in the next venture were wealthy relations of a former partner of J. P. Morgan of the well-known banking house in New York. This move proved a failure.[23] Disgusted, the men left Silver City and went to San Francisco.

Brockman dropped down to Deming one day, where he happened to be just in time to see a car of ore from a new place sampled, and to see the results of the assays. They were exceptionally good; he became intensely interested. Learning the locality, he lost no time in getting on the ground. He was successful in securing an option at what, to most mining men, would be considered a big price. He now burned the wires to his late partners to come and see what he had found. They were somewhat cold to his first request, but a second and very urgent wire persuaded them to come. It resulted in a deal, and turned out big enough to make millions for each of them.[24]

Brockman went to Los Angeles and invested in real estate. Some all-wise power seemed to have guided him, for his investments were all first class. He has now passed on, but he left behind an estate probated at three million dollars.[25] He got his start off the shoulders of Hartford M. Meredith[26] and Henry B. Ailman.

Epilog

After the failure of the Meredith and Ailman Bank, Harry Ailman faced the most difficult period of his life. When Meredith went to Washington, he left Harry to shoulder the full responsibility of straightening out their business affairs and trying to salvage something from the ruins. All the assets were tied up in litigation, and Harry still had a family to support. Once again he turned to mining and prospecting, hoping to find another Naiad Queen.

Ira Smith, Harry's father-in-law, owned a gold mine and a five-stamp mill at Pinos Altos. The mine had once been a good producer, but it was now closed down because of a problem with bad air. Harry spent several months trying to reactivate this mine, but he found that little could be done without money. In January 1889, he and Smith mortgaged the Pinos Altos property and took an option on the Trinidad gold mine near Clifton, Arizona. They planned to erect a stamp mill and make the property pay. The Trinidad did not turn out to be the bonanza that they expected. At the end of a year they were forced to shut down for lack of funds.

Harry now made two trips into Mexico to investigate the silver mines around Nacozari. Convinced that he had found something good, he returned to Silver City to seek capital for development. Once again he was disappointed. The market value of silver was now below $1.00 per ounce. The Mexican government had placed severe restrictions on foreign mining operations in Mexico. Times were hard, and no one was interested in risking their money on such an insecure proposition. Harry kept a journal of his trips to Mexico and later wrote the story of this adventure, probably planning to include it in his memoirs (see Appendix C).

In February 1892 the court cases which had tied up the Meredith and Ailman estate for so many years were finally resolved. The receiver was ordered to proceed with the settlement. In May of that year, Harry moved his family to Los Angeles, California, where he hoped to make a new start. He found economic conditions in Los Angeles at this time, however, no better than they were in Silver City, and jobs were scarce.

In looking around for something to do, Harry came across some old friends from New Mexico, C. A. Canfield and Edward L. Doheny, formerly of Kingston and Silver City. In later years he described the beginning of his new career as follows:

In the year 1892 the only thing in Los Angeles worthy of the name *oil* was several shallow holes about a hundred feet in depth on a ranch west of the city. The product was a heavy tar fit only for road building, but it was in demand for this purpose.

C. A. Canfield, an old acquaintance and at that time a partner of Edward L. Doheny, suggested the idea of sinking a shaft instead of a ten-inch drill hole, thereby allowing greater space for seepage of the thick stuff. With this idea in mind, Canfield and Doheny leased three lots just north of what was then known as Joe Byers Park, now nonexistent, but the location is one block north of the junction of West Second Street and the Glendale line.

I now learned of their plans, and finding the third lot was separated from the other two by several intervening lots, begged them to sublet that one to me. This was done and the digging started. Their company consisted of Canfield, Sam Cannon, and Doheny, and they were also the work force. I had only my father-in-law, my thirteen year old son, and myself. Their hoisting was a whip, while mine was a common windlass. The work was all done with pick and shovel; there was no blasting.

At a depth of sixty feet I began striking gas, the popping of which was frequently heard when a chunk of dirt was loosened. As depth was attained, this grew rapidly, and with it the seepage of oil far superior to the tar which we expected to have to be satisfied with. This attracted little attention, as nobody believed our holes would ever yield a worthwhile production.

When they had reached a depth of 140 feet and I 103 feet, I had much the best oil showing. We were now up against a snag that threatened to wreck both of us. It was the increasing gas. Canfield said that he could not stand the gas. He decided to give up his interest and go out on the desert to see if he could find something in a mining way. Cannon said he thought he could get his job in the bank back, and went there. Although quitting work, he was still friendly and willing to help if some way could be found other than going down in the hole to dig. Grandpa Smith told me that I was welcome to his share because he could not stand the gas. This blocked further progress as it clearly demonstrated the limit of our development with pick and shovel.

Doheny now came to me with an idea for drilling and proposed that I go in with him. Sam Cannon had some money that his parents left him, and he agreed to back the scheme. None of the rest of us could finance anything.

Their shaft being the deepest, it was selected. It had a timber or board partition in the center, adding another advantage. Our derrick had corner posts of four-by-four uprights, twenty-four feet long, with one-by-four braces. A redwood box with an eight inch clearance attached to the center partition gave us that much hole to start with. The drill was a rod of three-inch iron, shoved up at one end to permit attaching of a socket in which to insert a bit, fastened with a key. The bit was cross-shaped. A clevis was welded on the other end of the drill rod to take the rope on which the cable was spliced. The sand pump was made of a piece of five-inch casing about five feet long, installed and adjusted so as to carry the drill, but balanced and adjusted so a slight pull by our hands would make the drill hit bottom. Power was furnished by a borrowed horse.

Our rig was fully installed about March 1893. Doheny elected himself driller and, of course, I was assistant. My young son was anything he could do. The drill was lowered, or I should say run. The first round came off fine, but far from it the second. Having no brakes of any kind, Doheny depended on snubbing to lower the drill, as he was almost an expert on knots and loops with a rope. In the second instance it failed to hold, and down went our three-hundred pound drill as though shot out of a cannon. It buried plenty in that soft formation.

Ed knew where there was a windlass with a cog gearing that he thought would pull it out. It was secured and tried, but the drill failed to budge. Again he knew where there was a chain block that would do the trick. It was secured and installed. Still the drill did not budge. I now suggested that I go down there and dig it out. The hole, though not producing oil, was nevertheless plenty smeary. Securing a rubber coat, I descended on the ladder and went to work. In some two and a half hours I had it out. It was in over two and a half feet.

To use oil well language, we now began to make hole. In about a week we had some thirty feet. It was along in the afternoon, and everything was going fine when we began to hit something hard every time the drill went down. Knees and arms aching from long continued motion, Ed said, "Let's pull her out." We started to do this, and during the slow process we waited patiently, wondering what our drill bit would look like. About ten feet more and the drill showed up, but to our astonishment that ten feet was soaked in oil. It was trickling down on the drill and dripping off the bit back into the hole. We hit something hard, yes, but something soft as well.

In my own shaft operation, I had secured empty tallow barrels thrown away by the Southern Pacific Railroad. I had some eight or nine barrels full and as many more empties on hand. I suggested that we get them over there the next morning and see how much oil we had, and whether it was enough to fill all of them. After bailing oil the next day until mid-afternoon our barrels were all full and the bailer was still coming up full when lowered.

This was the first oil well in the city of Los Angeles. Because he later achieved fame and fortune, Doheny is remembered for this discovery, with no mention of the part Ailman played in the operation.

Ailman and Doheny sold their first well for $900 and invested in better equipment. They drilled three more wells in the Los Angeles area and several in Puente and Newhall. These first wells touched off an oil boom. Everyone who could afford to lease a piece of ground and erect drilling rigs joined the rush. Within a few years there were more than 500 wells pumping oil on a narrow tract of land west of downtown Los Angeles. So much oil was pumped out that by the end of 1899 the market was glutted and the price of a barrel of oil was less than the cost of producing it.

Ed Doheny had great faith in the oil industry and wanted to pick up all the leases on the market. Ailman did not have the money, or perhaps did not want to take the gamble. He sold out to Doheny who went on to become a multi-millionaire in the petroleum industry.

Harry continued working in the oil fields for several years. However, his real interest was still in mining. In 1900 he moved his family to Long Beach, California, and went to Nevada. After investigating mining conditions there and in northern California, he turned to Arizona where he acquired an interest in a copper property. He spent several years developing this, dividing his time between Arizona and his home in California. In 1928 he disposed of his copper mine and retired.

The *Silver City Enterprise*, September 30, 1938, carried the following item:

Judge W. A. Leonard, former editor of the *Enterprise*, sends us the following notation on the death of a pioneer of this section: "Henry B. (Harry) Ailman, aged 94 years, passed away at his home, Long Beach, California, September 16.

Deceased was one of the real pioneers of southern New Mexico, arriving at Silver City during the early 1870s. He was one of the discoverers of the Georgetown mines where he made a substantial fortune. He later engaged in the general mercantile and banking business in Silver City under the firm name of Meredith and Ailman. The firm was of material aid to miners, prospectors, and also to cattlemen and ranchers during pioneer days in the Southwest. When silver was demonetized by the Cleveland administration in 1883, followed later by three years of drouth, the firm of Meredith and Ailman, which had hundreds of thousands of dollars loaned to various industries, was compelled to suspend business, but all depositors of the bank were paid in full.

Deceased and family moved to Long Beach in 1892, where he resided until called to the Great Beyond. The surviving family consists of three daughters, two sons, and nine grandchildren, all residents of Long Beach, Mrs. Ailman having passed on several years ago.

Appendix A

Mrs. Ailman's Story

This autobiographical sketch, written by Theora Virginia Ailman in 1912, was included in Harry Ailman's papers. Mrs. Ailman died September 27, 1928, at the age of 72, at her home in Long Beach, California.

I was born in Quincy Branch County, Michigan, July 20, 1856. Three years later my parents moved to St. Louis, Missouri, where we lived for two years, then we moved to the town of Dawson, Illinois. Though a small town at the time, it had good schools, and my mother taught me my letters and numbers so I could read and count when I was five years old.

We lived in that place five years. I went to school or had private lessons all of the time so had reached advanced arithmetic and Latin at ten years of age. We then moved back to St. Louis, where I had private lessons for the next two years.

When I went to public school again it was in Wyandotte, Kansas. I had for my schoolmates the Wyandotte and Delaware Indian boys and girls, and good friends they were too, and fine scholars. We had fine times for two years, then we went to southern Kansas where I finished the public school course and studied the normal, intending to be a teacher.

But I had the fever and ague so bad I could never teach a term without interruption so gave it up.

In 1877 we went to New Mexico by wagon. There was quite a party of us, as several families in the surrounding country were going, some for one reason and some for another. Some like ourselves were tired of the fever and ague, and the many years of grasshoppers (we had just had them for three years in succession). One man was taking his wife, who was in the last stages of consumption, to a higher altitude, thinking to prolong her life. Some were going to the mines in Colorado, so all together there were quite a number of us.

We had some very pleasant days and some very trying ones. We had some horses stolen by Indians who had come into our camp one Sunday afternoon and seemed friendly and peaceful. We gave them lunch, and they slipped away in the evening and our horses with them.

We saw large herds of buffalo and had buffalo meat for days. We also saw many antelope and had some to eat. We saw many wild horses too. They would come quite close to ours, and we had to guard ours closely to keep them from going away with them.

Some days we traveled comfortably all day, and some days we could hardly move at all. We had a great amount of rain for nearly two months till we crossed the western boundary of Kansas and were in eastern Colorado, then it was dry all of the time and we got along better. Some of the party left us there, going to Denver. We turned south to Trinidad.

One family had had a case or two of scarlet fever before they started, but did not consider it contagious so had not cleansed their belongings properly. Just before we reached Trinidad, someone else in their family became sick. At first we did not know what the trouble was, so each did what they could to help, and we were all exposed to it. Mrs. White, the lady who had consumption, died first, then my sister Luthera died. They thought I would die, but somehow I did not. Then a beautiful little boy, the pride of his family, went next. We buried them all in the cemetery on the mountainside.

My father was a member of the Masonic Order, and so he found friends in our sorrow and trouble, though I think we would anyway, for I have never seen people in distress out here in this great west, but that every hand was outstretched to help them. We had to rest awhile to let the sick ones get well, for nearly everyone was sick. Father preached a very vigorous sermon on cleanliness, so we cleansed ourselves and everything we had so we would give no one else trouble.

After a while we went on our journey, sad and heavy hearted, but it was the only way. After crossing the Raton mountains going south, we were too early for the summer rains so had long drives without water; one of sixty miles, one of ninety, and one forty. We could not carry much, so traveled at night and gave our animals only a few swallows of water at a time, first washing their mouths with a cloth just wet. We got along very well, and did not lose any by thirst or fatigue, though the way seemed very long sometimes. We passed through some strange old ruins of a former civilization which we would like to have examined, but the people who were living in them were having smallpox of a malignant type. As we could not help them except with our sympathy, we moved on rapidly, for we feared contagion.

We stopped at last in the shadow of the Santa Rita mountain near the town of Silver City in Grant County, New Mexico. Georgetown, another mining camp, was nearby, and Pinos Altos was twelve miles away. Fort Bayard, four miles away, was a twelve-company post and supposed to protect us from Indian raids, but was really a farce, for they took good care of themselves and let the Indians steal our horses and sometimes children. Sometimes the Indians killed whole families and took what they liked and burned the houses. It seemed we had left one trouble to find another, but there was no turning back.

We made ourselves as comfortable as possible. We got a very good house on what was then the Santa Rita and Chino copper mines. It had then been worked for more than a hundred years with varying intermissions caused by changes in the government of Mexico. After it came into the possession of the U.S., the Indians were so troublesome that the work was stopped for long periods of time. Just then there was only a caretaker there. He was gald to rent us a house to have company. After we lived there for a year, I was married. Father and Mother lived there another year.

I went to Georgetown to live on the silver mine that my husband owned and worked. It was very interesting to me. We had a mill down on the Rio Mimbres, four miles away, where my husband's partner and wife lived. I used to help keep the books for the mine. My husband superintended the work at the mine; he had about forty men. The ore was good and silver was a good price, and though we were a long way from a railroad we made quite a reasonable profit. The business partner was a good mill man and looked after the milling and refining of the ore. We used to have it hauled from the mine to the mill with ox teams, three or four yoke of oxen to a wagon. I can hear the driver shouting to them yet when I think of those days.

We used to refine our silver to within three points of the mint in our little furnace, and send it to the U.S. mint in 300 pound bricks. I would put a cover of some kind over them when they lay on the floor of my sitting room. They were too heavy for anyone to carry off, but it was best not to have them too much in evidence.

There were four white women in Georgetown when I went there, and we were good friends. We are widely scattered now, and not all of us are living. My first baby came to me on the mine. We had been married fourteen months. Everything had gone well with us, except the Indians had stolen some horses from us and had taken all of father's horses except one riding horse. We were very happy. Our baby was the third white boy born in camp so we were the recipients of much kindly attention.

Many of our men were college men who came out west to get a start, and they were fine fellows. Our mail did not come very regularly, and so our magazines and eastern papers were sometimes two or three months late, but we got the news and passed it on to everyone else. We were quite well informed on the world's happening, if a little late.

The first time I went out with my baby, one of our men came after us saying the Indians were out up the canyon, so we turned back and went home. We had a good adobe house, so we thought we would be comparatively safe in it. Just as we reached it, the bullets began to rattle on the roof, and some of them struck the buggy top. We stopped just long enough to get a gun and some ammunition, and then went on into town. Our house had a shingle roof and might burn, while there were many in town that had mud roofs and were safer and could be easily fortified.

We spent the day in a rather excited state. I suppose there seemed to be too many men with guns around, or the Indians decided to go somewhere else. For some reason they went away, and when night came we went home. They never attacked us again at the mine, but they went up and down our valleys doing as they would, and the officers at the Fort just followed them at a convenient distance to avoid battle. We lost a great many cattle and horses, and it was unsafe to be out on the roads.

Some Philadelphia (Calumet and Hecla) men bought our mine, and we moved to Silver City, the supply town for all of the surrounding country and the county seat of Grant County. My husband and his partner bought a wholesale and retail merchandise establishment, paying $50,000 for real estate and stock on hand. We built good houses, and thought we would make our home there, for the climate was fine, and we had no fever and ague to fight.

New mines were being opened, and people were taking up ranches on the streams and bringing in cattle and sheep. Business was good except for the Indians. All seemed lovely, and we hoped the government would help us with the Indians, but the red tape between the frontiersman and Washington is of interminable length, as we found to our sorrow.

The railroad had not reached more than halfway down our territory so we still depended upon ox teams to bring in our supplies. When the Indians captured them and helped themselves to what they liked and burned the rest, as they did that spring, we had to do without. There was no flour or meal in town, or coffee or sugar, and all of the crackers were gone too. It was too early for fresh garden vegetables in that altitude so it was Mexican beans and meat mostly. When a wagon train did get through, men fought over a sack of flour. My husband had to promise one to each family while they lasted, hoping there would be enough to go around.

In spite of it all, our little town grew and prospered till the decline of silver. At first we used to get $1.20 per ounce of refined silver, but when it fell to 55 cents many of the mines closed. Copper was too low to mine with profit. We had several years of drought so that the cattle and sheep died for want of food and water. We met with appalling losses on every side.

There seemed nothing to do but go to a new place and see if it would be better. We closed out our business and came to California, and we have remained here now almost twenty years. My four oldest children were born in New Mexico, the two youngest in Los Angeles—in all three boys and three girls. We lived in Los Angeles for seven years and have now lived in Long Beach for almost thirteen.

Appendix B

Jerome Ailman's Letter from New Mexico

Six months after arriving in Silver City, Jerome Ailman wrote the following letter to the Port Royal (Pennsylvania) Times describing his journey by stagecoach from Albuquerque to Silver City. Mileage is somewhat exaggerated, perhaps because it seemed farther to an easterner making his first trip to the Southwest.

Silver City, N.M., Dec. 15, 1880

Mr. J. W. Speddy—Dear Sir:

Just six months ago today at seven o'clock on Monday morning, I took the coach at Albuquerque for the south. Stories of Indian outrages were numerous, and many of them by no means unfounded. The recent massacre had pretty effectually checked travel and I entered the coach alone. A short distance from the town the road crosses the river. The coach was conveyed across by means of a large flat-boat, pushed by Mexicans who waded the water. The shifting quick-sands so frequently change the bed of the stream that it is hardly safe to ford it.

A single glance ahead and to either side will give a pretty good idea of the scenery for the next hundred and fifty miles. The river winds along more like a stream that has lost its way among the sands, than like a real river. Its current, however, when one is close enough to observe it, is surprisingly swift. On each side are the inevitable sand hills, and beyond these, naked mountains obstruct the view.

Along the road are frequent Mexican villages, but they only serve to make the scenery more dreary; for a more cheerless, uninviting habitation than a common adobe house with flat roof, it would be hard to find.

The mountains, though sombre and barren, are interesting on account of the many peculiar shapes they assume. One which can be seen for many miles bears a close resemblance to a Monk's cowl; another near Mesilla, called the Organ Mountain, looks at a distance like an immense pipe organ. Its sides are entirely destitute of vegetation, and the white rocks of which they are composed glisten in the sunlight like polished metal. Others, again called mesas, have flat tops and perpendicular sides and appear like portions of the valley shot upward by some violent internal commotion.

At noon we reached the little town of Sabinal, and took on another passenger in the person of a young doctor on his way to Fort Craig, ninety miles distant, to see a patient. Think of sending ninety miles for a doctor. I hope, however, that my young medical friends will not infer from this that the valley of the Rio Grande is the newly fledged physicians eldorado—not at least until they first come and spy out the land. Another doctor had recently located at Socorro, thirty miles from Fort Craig, but my traveling companion, being the older resident, took the precedence.

In the evening we took on two more passengers, and during the night still another so that we were pretty well crowded. But by seven o'clock on Tuesday morning we reached Socorro, 80 miles from Albuquerque. Here all the passengers stopped except two, and they got off at Fort Craig at noon.

During the afternoon we again crossed the river and by evening reached Paraje, a dirty, forlorn little Mexican village.

The yielding sands all along the way thus far had made the ride very tiresome. At Paraje, however, the road leaves the river and enters the Jornada del Muerto (Journey of Death). Here the coach rolled along very smoothly. This valley is ninety miles long and runs parallel with the river, but separated from it by a chain of mountains. Until recently not a drop of water could be obtained throughout the entire ninety miles. Now there is a well and stage station in the middle of it. This station is the only house in the valley.

The prairie dog, seen almost everywhere along the last thousand miles of my trip, here furnished the only signs of animal existence; and the deceptive mirage doubtless in the early days caused many a weary traveler to hasten his steps that he might quench his thirst in the lake which he soon found receded as he advanced.

A stage driver had recently been killed here by Indians, and as a protection, slight indeed, in case of attack, we were furnished with a single soldier. At midnight we reached Martin's Well, and by seven o'clock on Wednesday morning, Point of Rocks, a stage station at the south end of the lonely jornada. At the latter place we should have had breakfast, but the surroundings had the peculiar power of satisfying the appetite without the necessity of eating.

The first evidence the approaching stranger had of his nearness to a human habitation was a swarm of flies that literally covered everything. As the stage drove up, these arose into the air for a moment and disclosed a scene—but my pen falters, and as the driver has finished his lunch, and fresh horses have taken the place of tired ones, we will leave the place, glad that our stay is not necessarily longer.

And good reader, by the time you have occasion to pass that way, the dilapidated stage station, with its more than filthy surroundings will be as all stage stations are rapidly becoming, supplanted by a neat railroad depot, for the grader and the track layer build more rapidly than I write, and already passengers take the cars at Martin's Well, 180 miles south of where I left them six months ago.

At Point of Rocks our escort left us, and from there to Mesilla, the driver was my only companion. After riding a short distance, we once more came in sight of the Rio Grande; and the remainder of our road to Mesilla lay through the Mesilla valley.

Here the country is more thickly settled than any place I saw since leaving eastern Kansas. One can hardly resist the impression, however, that he has suddenly been thrown amidst the scenes of the Nile thousands of years in the past. Here is a fertile valley seldom visited by rains, but watered by ditches from the Rio Grande. In yonder field some four or five swarthy Mexicans are cutting grain with sickles; a little farther on, another is cleaning wheat by tossing it into the air and allowing the wind to drive the chaff away. The threshing floor is a smooth plot in the corner of his field, and the grain has been threshed by the hoffs of oxen and goats.

That ox-cart is certainly made after the pattern of those used in the time of Pharaoh; and I should not be surprised to learn that those donkeys are the lineal descendants of the ass that once talked to Balaam.

As we drew near to Mesilla an occasional vineyard still more forcibly brought to mind the scenes of the Bible. The luxuriant foliage and thick green clusters gave promise of a rich vintage in due season; but the ancient wine press had doubtless given place to one of more modern construction.

About two o'clock on Wednesday afternoon the coach drove into Mesilla, and there I had to stop until the following morning. Although this town, like all others on the Rio

Grande, is built of flat-roofed adobes, and its streets and side walks are nothing but dusty roads, yet its appearance is much less repulsive to the eye of the passing stranger, because of the large cottonwood trees on the public plaza, and the gardens and orchards on the outskirts.

But weariness soon put me to sleep in the evening, and desire to get to my journey's end made me impatient for the coach to start next morning. Sometime after seven o'clock on Thursday morning, a light wagon conveyed passengers and luggage down to the river a short distance from the town, and after considerable delay, we were ferried to the coach in waiting on the opposite side. Although the country seemed as dry as if it had never been visited by rain, yet the river was rising. This of course, was caused by the melting snows far to the north.

Our course, which had been south for the last 600 miles, now turned directly west, and another 100 miles would complete my journey. This was by far the most dangerous portion of the route, and had recently become little less than a gauntlet. There was but one house in the first fifty miles, and very few in the remaining fifty. Two soldiers as escorts accompanied us here, and there was one passenger besides myself.

Although we were now traveling directly across spurs of the Rocky Mountains, the passes are so wide that it is nearer the truth to call them plains, with mountains near at hand. At a few places the road leads through narrow canyons. Here the soldiers climbed the hillsides to look for Indians, but fortunately for us, found none.

Sometime during the forenoon, we passed a lot of dead cattle lying in a heap by the roadside. Near them was a pile of stones surmounted by a rude cross. Upon inquiry, we were informed that the cattle had been killed by Indians a short time before, and that the stones and the cross marked the death scene and resting place of eleven Mexicans who had fallen in the affray.

By sundown we arrived at Fort Cummings. Here there were several more passengers to get on the coach, and we were crowded during the night. A short distance beyond the fort, the road enters Cook's Canyon. More Indian outrages have been committed in this canyon than perhaps in any other spot in the territory.

We had not gone far, when a groan from an old man at my side indicated, as I afterwards learned, that we were passing the place where but a few days before, the Indians had killed his son. At the time that this young man lost his life, the coach was also taken, as [were] two men who happened to be passing in a wagon. There were no passengers in the coach however. Appearances indicated that the driver, after being made a prisoner, was burned at the stake, the ruins of his vehicle having been used to feed the flames.

Not far from this place our nostrils were greeted by the fetid odor of decaying flesh, and we were informed that it arose from the bodies of unburied Indians who had been killed shortly after the tragedy just mentioned. Not long after my arrival in Silver City the coach was again attacked, some distance beyond Fort Cummings, and the driver and two passengers left dead by the roadside.

I presume, however, that every reader knows that Victorio and his band, after these depredations, retired to Old Mexico, and that there he and a large portion of his followers met, at the hands of Mexican soldiers, the fate they had so often during the last two years, meted out to white men. The few who remain are doubtless scattered and no one apprehends any danger from them.

Moreover, by the time spring fairly opens, the railroads will be so near to Silver City that stage travel will be practically ended. But by daylight the stage drove into Fort Bayard and nine miles further on I caught the first glimpse of Silver City.

Published in the
Port Royal [Pennsylvania] *Times,*
February 3 and 10, 1881

Appendix C

Harry Ailman's Prospecting Trip to Mexico

During the years we were passing through our troubles, there lived in Silver City a wealthy sea captain whose name was David A. Martin. He owned a large herd of cattle and a ranch in the western part of Grant County near the Carlisle gold mine. His son managed the ranch while Captain Martin, with his wife and two daughters, lived in town. Martin, still in vigorous health and with much leisure time on his hands, often sought a companion, packed several animals, and made prospecting trips. On one such trip into the Sierra Madre Mountains of Mexico, he had come upon an abandoned silver mine which looked like a very promising prospect. One day in the fall of 1891, I met Captain Martin downtown, and he suggested that I accompany him to relocate this mine. Of course, I was open for something along that line and at once became interested and decided to go.

We left Silver City the 27th of October. Our route lay through the Burro Mountains and across the big prairie north of Lordsburg, a station on the Southern Pacific Railroad. We reached Stein's Pass on the fourth day. On finding the grass very short here, we made a hard drive on to the headquarters ranch of the San Simon Cattle Company. As Captain Martin was acquainted with Scott White, the owner, we received a hearty welcome and an invitation to turn our animals into a fenced up pasture and dine with him. White's herd consisted of thirty thousand head of cattle, but there was neither butter or milk on his table and few vegetables. We had potatoes, corn bread, and plenty of what Texas people called sow belly. This means no criticism, but merely shows the Texas idea of a meal.

The ranch was on the San Simon River which flowed north and emptied into the Gila. At this point the river was from one to two hundred feet underground. To get this water where the herd could reach it, a string of windmills were installed with earthen reservoirs having banks seven to eight feet high. At the time of our visit, there was not a drop of water in any of them. Plenty of animals stood by, waiting patiently for a chance to drink, while the biggest bull in the lot stood with his nose against the discharge pipe to catch the few drops that would come at a now-and-again turn of the windmill. He would hold his place till satisfied, if it took a whole afternoon. Younger animals by the half-dozen lay dead nearby, starved for water. I wondered at a man with the intelligence of Scott White permitting such a condition to exist.

Now nearing the boundary between the United States and Mexico, we sighted a herd of nineteen antelope. Not being in a position to take care of fresh meat, we did not frighten them with the crack of our rifles. We passed by a little distance away in a gulch, so they could only see our heads bobbing. Soon after passing, I looked back and within 150 feet stood the big buck of the bunch peering over the brink at us. It was a magnificent shot, but I resisted the temptation.

The next day brought us to Rancho San Bernadino, owned by John Slaughter. Here old mother nature once ran a volcano of respectable size, leaving behind a large black mesa [tableland] of many acres. At the western terminal a beautiful spring of wholesome water sprang forth. The flow irrigated acres of grassland, always green. Early-day Spaniards established a mission here for conversion of the Indians. My experience with said Indians was that the mission made but little headway in converting them. The remains of the mission buildings were still visible at the time of our visit. A large monument of stone, south of the ranch, marked the boundary lines. Here I found it was possible to plant one foot in the United States and the other in Mexico.

Now in Mexico, our next town was Fronteras, some distance ahead. The only inhabited spot we passed was a Mexican distillery where they made a drink called *tiswin* out of a species of native cactus grown on the nearby hills. I knew what old frontier forty-rod whiskey was, but the Mexican product beat it a mile. That stuff would burn the soles off your shoes.

The Mexican custom house was then located at Fronteras. As our prospecting outfit had nothing to pay duties on, we decided to avoid both the town and custom examinations by keeping off the trail in the brush until four or five miles below the town. After making camp for the night on the Fronteras River, we heard a strange noise that sounded like a hog in distress. I appeared on the roadside to investigate. Here came a Mexican, mounted on a burro, dragging a good size hog by a long rope tied to one of its hind legs. Of course, in that excitable condition, the hog was dead by the time the Mexican reached his ranch.

Our course the next day was about due south along what seemed to be the only public wagon road in that part of the country. During the day we passed four or five big American wagon trains going north loaded with concentrates from the San Pablo mines. Settlements were few and a considerable distance apart, but here was the finest grazing country for stock ranching I ever saw, with red bunch grass a foot or more high and miles and miles of it. This splendid grass country, not yet occupied by large cattle ranches, was an ideal home for deer. It was a daily occurrence to see herds of a dozen or more. There was also plenty of oak timber in this region.

Three days from Fronteras brought us to the home of P. W. Smith, an old friend of Captain Martin. This was a lovely cool place, among cottonwoods and sycamore, located on the Nacozari River which was quite a lovely stream at this point. We now learned that a party had passed through here a month ago with the object of locating the same property we were after. That, of course, knocked us out of that proposition. To help us in our disappointment, Smith introduced us to John Hohstein, one of his employees who had a so-called "big mine" up his sleeve. His story was as follows: A smuggler, and there were many in those days, coming south with several heavily packed animals, took to the mountains, regardless of any trail, in order to avoid meeting custom house officers on the road. In so doing, he came upon an old abandoned mine with a large dump which indicated considerable development. The smuggler was in no shape to make an examination at the time and would not tell anyone where the mine was. John Hohstein was an expert at trailing, which was a necessary accomplishment in that country. He back tracked the smuggler, although there were places on the rocks where a few scratches were all he had to guide him. Determination and perseverence won, and he found the mine. He was now willing to guide us to said mine without charge.

We made an early start the next day, using the main road for part of the way. We passed through a place called San Miguelita where the ore from nearby mines was treated. This mining was started in the sixteenth and seventeenth centuries while Jesuit churches generally prevailed. The ruins indicated there was once quite a population here. Transportation was exclusively by burros in those days and not even a wagon road existed. Machinery made of iron or steel could not be gotten there by any means. Rocks and oak trees were the only materials available, and of these were constructed the arastras, many of them some twenty feet in diameter. They had blasting powder, but at times it ran short. I saw drill holes which had been filled with lime, burned, and then water inserted hoping the expansion would crack the rock. What I saw indicated these tactics usually failed. Old smelting furnaces were here in goodly number, and pieces of exceedingly rich ore were still lying around.

Our course was now off the wagon road and into the hills. We entered a valley and took a course across a dry lake, but we soon found it not so dry as we had been led to believe. I was following Captain Martin who usually bore the scales down close to two hundred pounds. His riding burro was stout, but only of medium size. Anyone knowing a burro's habits, knows he has no use for soft mud. The mud became softer. Martin's burro was about to mire down, with Martin urging him on with all his persuasive powers and a little hot language, to keep from being compelled to get off in a foot or more of alkali mud. I enjoyed the scene, but dared not laugh out loud for it would certainly have riled Martin's feelings. He escaped, but it was a close call. I had a bigger animal and made it easily.

After some four miles of rough mountain climbing we arrived at the mine in the late afternoon. Tired and with appetites somewhat whetted, we had supper and turned in for the night. The next morning I proceeded to examine the old mine. The works indicated extreme age. I could only explore about forty feet of the tunnel because ahead of that it was dangerous from long standing. I found the vein, about ten to twelve feet wide, but much of it was too low grade to yield any profit with the facilities I have already described for treating the ore. Their places for assorting were still visible. These I examined carefully and succeeded in gathering possibly a pound of particles, none larger than a grain of corn, which I packed carefully to assay when I got home. We examined the country as to getting in and out with wagons, and found it would be easy.

On the return trip by a different route, Captain Martin got off another stunt. Climbing the side of a long slope, he saw a fine specimen of quail. As I was behind, he signaled me to wait. He dismounted and with a stick the size of a walking cane approached quietly. The quail, unmoving, watched him. Bang with the stick and over toppled the bird. Martin said it was a fool quail, and I thought it well named.

Arriving back at the Smith home, we made a careful examination of his excellent collection of gold and silver specimens collected from the surrounding country. We then arranged to spend the next two days making trips to other mining properties. Following a course south, we passed through the village of Nacozari. Here was once a Jesuit Mission of considerable importance, but it was now in ruins. Within one hundred feet stood the New Jersey Yankie's San Pedro concentrating mill. They drew their ores from the San Pedro mine which, according to the records, was famous as a producer during the palmy days of the said church. From Nacozari we proceeded due east six miles to the San Pedro mine. On the same vein another American company operated the San Pablo mine. They had reached a depth of three hundred feet, and were constructing a very fine mill.

Satisfied that we had at least found a very interesting mining country, we started for home November 21, over the same route followed coming in. We arrived home December 3. The entire trip of some six hundred miles had required thirty-eight days and was one of the most pleasant and interesting prospecting trips I ever had anything to do with.

I had the samples which I brought from Mr. Hohstein's mine assayed, and they showed a silver value of six hundred ounces to the ton. The assaying was done by a prominent mining company operating properties in and near Silver City. The company was so interested in the results that they agreed to send us back with their assayer, Mr. Brown, to locate the mine and make a more thorough exploration.

For this second trip we were supplied with a buckboard, large enough to accommodate three men and their necessary baggage, drawn by a handsome span of dark brown mules. This meant we had to follow the wagon road, with no dodging the custom house at Fronteras. Mr. Brown and Captain Martin spoke no Spanish, and I spoke only a little, but did understand more than either of them. I was delegated to negotiate our permit to pass. The duties on an outfit such as ours, if paid in full, would come to some sixty dollars provided we intended to remain permanently. However, for a simple prospecting trip such as ours, they had a scheme like this: a party at Fronteras made a business of going security for our return within a certain number of days. His fee was nine dollars Mexican money. This was arranged, the custom house satisfied, and we received permission to pass through.

Returning to our rig where Brown and Martin awaited me, I found that a third party had joined them. This was a handsome Mexican named Eduardo Baca who had been educated in California and spoke good English. Baca had a fine specimen of bornite copper ore, on which my opinion was requested. I said it looked good and asked where it came from.

His reply was, "I have a store here and staked two prospectors. This is what they found in a range of mountains to the west called Monte San Jose." Further conversation led to an agreement to stop over on our way back and go to see this place.

Continuing our journey, three days later we again arrived at the Smith ranch. From there we went on to Oposura, the town where the mining records are kept. Reaching this town in late afternoon, we found an American doctor, with a Mexican wife, who kindly allowed us to camp in his corral. He said we could water our animals in the acequia [irrigation ditch] on the other side of the plaza, and it fell to my lot to water the mules. As I walked across the vacant square in the center of the town, the thought came to my mind that there was not a human being outside of my own party who knew me in that place. Suddenly a voice sang out, "Hello, Harry. Where in hell did you come from?" Looking around, I saw it was Bill Brock whom I had known in Pinos Altos. He had shot and killed a chinaman in that town and was down there as a fugitive from justice. I had quite a visit and gained some information from him. I learned that another party had already denounced [located] the John Hohstein property since our former trip. We were knocked out again.

We now retraced our steps and in due time arrived at Fronteras where Eduardo Baca awaited us. He was the son of a wealthy family which owned an extensive, well stocked, cattle ranch thirty miles long and almost as many wide. Eduardo had a wife and two children. He operated a general store in Fronteras and owned a home there. We were invited to camp in his corral and to partake of a meal with him and his family. As he was well able financially to have all the comforts a family would enjoy, I was surprised to see their living room, where they also slept. The wife and children used a dried cow hide spread on the floor for a mattress, while he occupied a no-spring lounge with a thin mattress. I write this simply to show their idea of home comforts. I have seen several other cases very similar.

The following morning, with Mr. Baca as guide, we were off to see his mine, some twenty odd miles away in a mountainous country. We arrived in the late afternoon and camped for the night on a lively running creek at the foot of the hill on which is located the prospect. This permanent water and a good stand of oak timber looked good. The creek was of sufficient size to furnish water power for a small feed-grinding mill three or four miles below the mine.

We looked the mine over. The ore vein was in a contact between a lime formation and porphyry. It was three to ten feet wide and had been developed by a thirty-foot shaft and two open cuts some hundred feet apart. Brown and I took several samples, the best being of the same character as what Baca showed us at the custom house in town. He offered us this prospect for twelve hundred dollars Mexican money.

We once again returned to Silver City, and the assay office of Mr. Brown, to find out what values this ore carried. The poorest sample, which we thought was iron, assayed sixteen ounces silver; the best assayed one hundred and ten ounces silver and two ounces, or forty dollars, gold. This was exactly the same kind of ore that the Cooney mine had produced, the handling of which I was well posted.

These assays showed me that here was the opportunity I had been hunting ever since our downfall at Silver City four years ago. At that time, silver ranged at close to a dollar per ounce and copper from fourteen to sixteen cents per pound, with the United States government buying four million ounces fine silver per month for coinage purposes. In 1892, when Grover Cleveland was the Democrat nominee for president, he gave out this slogan, "If I am elected, I will call congress together and request the repeal of that silver purchase clause." He was elected and kept his promise, knocking silver down to fifty three cents per ounce. Now nothing in my ore was attractive but the gold, and that of itself was not enough. Cooney, during the years 1885, '86 and '87, piled up a profit of over $600,000. Now I, with a better proposition for permanency, couldn't interest capital to touch it—all brought about by politics. Why, oh why, could not fate have permitted me to find this three years sooner?

Footnotes

Chapter 1

1.   Ancestors of Harry Ailman came to the United States from Germany. They settled at Newport, Rhode Island, where his grandfather, Frederick, was born in 1766. Sometime after 1800 Frederick moved his family to York County, Pennsylvania, where Harry's father, David, was born in 1805. Frederick served in the war of 1812, and in 1816 he moved his family to Juniata County, Pennsylvania. Harry was the first of six children born to David and Amelia Ailman. *Second U.S. Census*, 1800, Newport County, Rhode Island; Genealogy notes from Ailman memoirs.

2.   The Pennsylvania Railroad was incorporated in April 1846, to build a line from Philadelphia to Pittsburg. After this line was completed in 1858, the purchase or lease of several small lines extended the Pennsylvania to Lake Michigan and Chicago, St. Louis and Cincinnati. Stewart H. Holbrook, *The Story of American Railroads*, pp. 81–83.

3.   Kansas took a liberal view toward women's sufferage, consequently it was dubbed "The Paradise of Petticoats." The state also had advanced thoughts on education, with a school in every small settlement of a dozen or more houses. William A. Bell, *New Tracks in North America*, p. 15.

4.   The Kansas Pacific Railroad, a subsidiary of the Union Pacific, was chartered as the Leavenworth, Pawnee, and Western by the state of Kansas in 1855. It was given a large grant of land to build a branch line from the mouth of the Kansas River to a junction with the Union Pacific near the hundredth meridian. Construction did not get underway until 1863. The following year the name was changed to Union Pacific Eastern Division. In 1866 the proposed route was extended into

Colorado to join the main line not more than fifty miles from Denver. As this addition made the Eastern Division more a through line than a branch line, in 1869 the name was changed to the Kansas Pacific. Robert Edgar Riegel, *The Story of Western Railroads*, pp. 112–14.

5.   The Missouri, Kansas, and Texas (Katy) Railroad was originally chartered as the Union Pacific Southern Branch to build a line southward to the Gulf of Mexico. In 1870 it reached the southern boundary of Kansas and early in 1873 the line was completed to Denison, Texas, where connections were made with the Houston and Texas line to the Gulf. Ibid. p. 108.

6.   Kit Carson, Colorado, named after the famous frontiersman, was a supply and trading post in the 1860s. When the westward-building Kansas Pacific railroad crossed the eastern Colorado border, the construction headquarters was moved from Sheridan, Kansas, to Kit Carson. After the railroad was completed, Kit Carson was the terminus for freight, mail, and passengers bound for New Mexico and southern Colorado until a branch line was built to Las Animas in 1873. Morris F. Taylor, *First Mail West*, p. 137.

7.   The buffalo were essential to the Indian's way of life. In addition to furnishing them with food, the skins were used for clothing, robes and shelter; implements and utensils were made from the horns and bones; and dried buffalo chips were used for fuel on the treeless plains. Buffalo Bill Cody, who supplied meat for the construction crews on the Kansas Pacific Railroad, claimed to have killed 4,280 buffalo in less than eight months. Don Russell, *The Lives and Legends of Buffalo Bill*, pp. 88–89.

8.   May 14, 1870, a few weeks before Harry Ailman arrived at Kit Carson, the Kansas Pacific construction crews were raided by several small bands of Indians who struck simultaneously at different points along the line. Eleven men were killed, ten were wounded, and four hundred head of company stock were stolen. Troops from Fort Wallace were sent to patrol the area and protect the crews. *The Rocky Mountain News*, May 14, 1870.

9.   There was friendly rivalry between the construction crews building westward under Colonel E. W. Weed and those working out of Denver supervised by L. H. Eichollz. On the last day, with ten and a quarter miles of track to lay, a large American flag was raised midway of the distance and the crews were challenged to race for the prize. Work began at 5:00 A.M., and the flag was taken at 1:10 P.M. by Colonel Weed's force. The last spike was driven home at 3:00 P.M., completing the

line from Kansas City and St. Louis to Denver. *The Rocky Mountain News*, August 16, 1870.

10. The construction company provided a fine celebration dinner for the crews. The meal included such special items as ice cream, California fruit, champagne, and cigars. Ibid.

11. At first the engineers thought they could outrun the buffalo herds, which often contained several hundred animals. A few accidents taught them that hitting one of the massive creatures could derail the engine. At times a train was held up for several hours waiting for the stampeding herd to get clear of the tracks. Everett Dick, *Vanguards of the Frontier*, p. 432.

12. An estimated ten million buffalo roamed the Great Plains in 1865. As the railroads advanced toward the west, buffalo hunting became such a popular sport that the railroad companies offered special excursions to the buffalo grounds. This attracted hunters and sportsmen by the thousands. There was also great demand for buffalo robes, and professional hunters and frontiersmen joined in the wholesale slaughter. By the mid 1880s the great buffalo herds were almost extinct. Ibid, 432–42.

Chapter 2

1. The discovery of gold brought a rush to Colorado in 1859. This was followed by a period of depression a few years later as the placers, never very extensive, played out and the gold lodes were found to contain refractory ores requiring costly milling machinery and new techniques for amalgamation. Although silver mining in Colorado began in a small way toward the end of the 1860s, prospecting and development were so vigorously pursued that Colorado produced over a million dollars in silver bullion in 1871. Rodman Wilson Paul, *Mining Frontiers of the Far West*, pp. 109–124.

2. The Little Colorado River rises in the White Mountains of Arizona, near the central portion of the Arizona-New Mexico boundary. It winds its way north and west, carving out an impressive gourge before tumbling into the Grand Canyon to join the mighty Colorado River.

3. Stephen Percy Robbin claimed to be a merchant from San Francisco. Richard Morton Cole, from Burlington, Vermont, styled himself a mining engineer. Within a month of their arrival in southwestern New Mexico these two had located some fifteen mining claims, none of

which proved to be of value. They soon moved on in search of richer prospects. *Grant County Mining Records*, Book 18, pp. 742–57. John Edward Comerford, from Cataraqui, Ontario, Canada, became a permanent resident of Grant County. For several years he ran a saloon on Bullard Street. In 1874 he joined a group of homesteaders bound for the Gila Valley. He took up land on Duck Creek for farming and ranching, calling it Cataraqui Place after his former home in Canada. Ed Comerford met with a tragic end in August 1880, when he was brutally murdered by Epifano Munos, a horse thief. *The Daily Southwest*, August 17, 18, 19, 1880.

4.   The country south of Kit Carson was made up of miles of rolling sand hills cut by an occasional dry arroyo. Getting stuck was a common occurrence. Freighters often doubled up their teams, putting as many as twenty yoke of oxen to a wagon in order to pull through a particularly bad stretch. P. G. Scott, "Diary of a Freighting Trip From Kit Carson to Trinidad in 1870," *The Colorado Magazine*, Vol. 8 (1930):147–49.

5.   Kiowa Ranch was probably Kiowa Springs Station, a stage stop midway between Kit Carson and the Arkansas River on the main wagon road leading into southwestern Colorado and New Mexico. Morris F. Taylor, *First Mail West*, p. 131.

6.   Fort Lyon was located on the north bank of the Arkansas River about two and one-half miles below the mouth of the Purgatoire River. The original post, Fort Wise, was established in 1860 to protect the northern route of the Santa Fe Trail and located some twenty miles to the east. Two years later the name was changed to honor General Nathaniel Lyon, early casualty of the Civil War. In 1867 flood damage and unhealthy conditions necessitated moving the fort to the new site on a bluff high above the river. Leo E. Oliva, *Soldiers on the Santa Fe Trail*, pp. 126–30, 175–78.

7.   Across the Arkansas from Fort Lyon was the village of Las Animas, named for the Rio de Las Animas (Purgatoire River) which flows into the Arkansas nearby. Founded in 1869, Las Animas soon became a supply point for freight and stage traffic from the railroad up the Arkansas valley to Pueblo or south into New Mexico. Kenyon Riddle, *Records and Maps of the Old Santa Fe Trail*, pp. 37–38.

8.   The Purgatoire River is the most important tributary of the upper Arkansas. The Spanish name for the stream was *Rio de Las Animas Perdidas*. The French version was *Purgatoire*, which the Anglos pronounced "Picketwire." Ibid. p. 37.

9.   Hiram J. Hutchinson had a very diversified career during his lifetime. He was born in Troy, New York, October 1, 1836, and went to sea as a young boy. After a few years he returned to New York where he went into business, married, and raised a family. Following the Civil War, he was captain of one of the largest boats on the Great Lakes for several years before joining the prospecting party. After Hutchinson came to New Mexico he lived in Silver City for a year, prospecting throughout the surrounding area for silver and gold, then moved to Central City, New Mexico, where he spent the rest of his life. He opened a general mercantile store, ran a saloon, and at various times served as deputy sheriff, justice of the peace, and school commissioner. He owned a cattle ranch, develop mining claims in Mogollon and Central, and in 1887 was appointed the first postmaster of Central. Hiram Hutchinson died April 15, 1899, at the age of sixty-three. *Silver City Enterprise,* April 21, 1899.

10.   The party was now following a wagon trail established in the early 1860s by Madison Emery. From Las Animas, Colorado, the route went south and slightly east then swung to the southwest, skirting the west end of Mesa de Maya and heading directly south through Emery Gap, a natural and easy passage from Colorado into New Mexico. Riddle, *Records and Maps of the Old Santa Fe Trail,* Map sheet 2.

11.   A large volcanic province extends from northeastern New Mexico into the southeastern portion of Colorado. There are more than a hundred extinct volcanoes in this region, and much of the area is covered by lava flows or *malpais,* cinder piles and volcanic centers. Wm. R. Muehlberger, Brewster Baldwin, and Roy W. Foster, *High Plains Northeastern New Mexico.*

12.   After passing through Emery Gap and what is now called Toll Gate Canyon, the trail dropped into the Dry Cimarron Valley. James Madison Emery discovered this valley in 1862 while searching for a good wagon road between Colorado and northeastern New Mexico, and established the first settlement in the valley in 1864. Emery came west from Ohio as a young man, trapping, hunting, and trading with the Indians and hauling military supplies under government contract. After the discovery of gold in Colorado, he made his headquarters at Denver where he met and married Mrs. Susan Sumpter in 1861. The Emerys moved to New Mexico, accepting Lucien B. Maxwell's offer of 160 acres of farmland to anyone who would settle on the Maxwell Land Grant. Emery continued freighting for the government and sold much of his

farm produce to markets in Denver. In 1864 Madison Emery and several others took up land in the Dry Cimarron Valley, establishing farms and ranches. The settlement, consisting of a store, blacksmith shop, grist mill, and a few homes, became the village of Madison, named after its founder. Sometime in later years Emery left home because of family trouble, coming eventually to Grant County where he died in 1891. Biographical information from the family records, courtesy of William L. Emery, Clayton, New Mexico.

13. Numerous extinct volcanoes rise from the gently rolling plains of northeastern New Mexico. Capulin Mountain National Monument, the most perfectly preserved example of a cinder cone, is in this area. Ailman and his party were now on the Fort Leavenworth-Fort Union freight road which passed about a mile to the east of Capulin.

14. Sam Green, from Kenosha, Wisconsin, was a mechanic by trade. he is said to have helped organize the Wisconsin-Silver City Mining Company which brought one of the first stamp mills to Silver City in 1872, and was superintendent of the Wisconsin mill for a time. In 1877 he was associated with Tom Lyons in the building of a quartz mill at Globe, Arizona. He was superintendent of several mills in and around Silver City during his career, and was considered one of the most competent mill men in the area. He died in Pinos Altos, February 17, 1891, during a severe epidemic of "La Grippe," or influenza.

15. The Red River is also called the Canadian River. In 1845 Kit Carson and Richard Owens established a ranch about fifty-five miles east of Taos on the Little Cimarron River which flows east then south to form the Canadian River. They sold the ranch six months later to join the Frémont expedition to California. In 1849 Carson established another ranch with Lucien B. Maxwell at Rayado. Both places were too far west to have been on the route traveled by Ailman. Harvey Lewis Carter, *Dear Old Kit*, pp. 95–123.

16. The village referred to was probably Gallinas Springs, shown on the Wheeler map of 1876 but no longer in existence. It was on the direct route of the Santa Fe Trail on which the party was now traveling. Gallinas Springs was within the boundaries of the Mora Land Grant where a number of settlers had established villages. They farmed small tracts of land, finding a ready market for grain, produce, sheep, and goats at Fort Union and with travelers along the trail. Letter from Dr. Myra Ellen Jenkins, Historical Services Division, State Records Center and Archives, Santa Fe, New Mexico, June 17, 1976.

17.   Early visitors from the east were fascinated by the Mexican cart and plow. James F. Meline, who toured New Mexico in 1866, described the plow as "a monumental affair, with wood-work enough in it to furnish the rafters of a small house." It had a heavy beam, some sixteen feet long, with a small forked piece of wood attached. The two-wheeled cart was made of crudely fashioned pieces of wood held together with strips of rawhide. For each wheel, a thick, oblong block of wood was fastened by wooden pegs between two halves of a circle. The axle-tree was attached through a hole in the center of each wheel. As no grease was used on the axle, the progress of the carts could be heard some distance away. James F. Meline, *Two Thousand Miles on Horseback,* pp. 158–59.

18.   Fort Union was located on a treeless plain twenty-six miles northeast of Las Vegas, New Mexico. It was established in 1851 as a central supply and troop depot for military operations in the Southwest. The garrison stationed here was charged with maintaining peace among the Indian tribes of the area and furnishing an escort for wagon trains traveling on the Santa Fe Trail. In 1871 Fort Union was a four-company post laid out on two sides of a rectangular parade ground. The single-story territorial style buildings were of adobe, built on stone foundations and topped with brick coping and flat tin roofs. There was a vast collection of workshops, warehouses, corrals and stables, a large shingle-roofed hospital and a well-stocked sutler's store. Oliva, *Soldiers on the Santa Fe Trail,* pp. 178–80.

19.   Tipton's store was on the Santa Fe Trail about five miles south of Fort Union. William B. Tipton was born in Columbia, Missouri, and came to New Mexico as a freighter in 1846. He went to work for Samuel B. Watrous, moving, in 1849 to the vicinity of La Junta (now Watrous), New Mexico, at the junction of the Mora and Sapello Rivers where Watrous owned a large parcel of land in the Scolly Grant. Tipton acquired land two miles north of La Junta, developed a good farm, married a daughter of Sam Watrous, built a fine home, and opened a store along the Santa Fe Trail. The village which grew up around the store was known as Tiptonville. George P. Hammond, *The Adventures of Alexander Barclay, Mountain Man,* p. 211. Gregg's Tavern at La Junta offered meals and lodging to the traveler, and was a popular stopping place along the Santa Fe Trail. George W. Gregg, the owner, had a farm in the valley and was married to another daughter of Sam Watrous. George

was the first postmaster of La Junta, appointed 1868. Taylor, *First Mail West*, p. 148.

20.   Las Vegas, New Mexico, was an important trade center and stop-over on the Santa Fe Trail. The area known as the *Vegas Grandes* was first settled in 1833, when land bordering on the Rio Gallenas was granted to a group of settlers and the community known as *Nuestra Senora De Las Vegas* (Our Lady of Sorrows of the Meadows) was founded. T. M. Pearce, *New Mexico Place Names*, pp. 85–86.

21.   Enoch Warrington, thirty-one years old and a stonemason by trade, came from Aurora, Illinois. His twenty-five year old brother, Nelson, was also a member of the prospecting party. After arriving in New Mexico, the Warrington brothers located several promising mining claims in Grant County and homesteaded a farm in the Gila Valley. In 1879 they sold the farm, and Enoch returned to Illinois where he died in 1884. Nelson moved to Silver City and opened the Pioneer Corral and Livery Stable on Broadway, operating a stage line from Silver City to Georgetown and another running to Paschal. In 1884 he moved his livery stable to Tombstone, Arizona, where he soon went bankrupt. He returned to New Mexico, homesteaded a ranch two miles east of Lordsburg, and developed mining property at Pyramid. Nelson suffered several paralytic strokes in the early 1900s. He was placed in the Territorial Insane Asylum, but was later moved to the Soldier's Home in Los Angeles, California, where he died in 1910.

22.   Anton Chico is located thirty-two miles south of Las Vegas at the southern edge of the Sangre de Cristo Mountains. It was founded by Don Salvador Tapia and sixteen others who received this tract as a land grant in 1822. The village, situated on high ground along the west bank of the Pecos River, was divided into the upper and lower plaza typical of many early Mexican settlements. Anton Chico was built to withstand hostile Indian raids, with high walls enclosing stone and adobe houses and sturdy rock and pole corrals. Betty Shouse, "Anton Chico, Historic Village," *New Mexico Magazine*, Vol. 37 (1959):3–6.

23.   The route to Albuquerque ascended for some thirty miles from Anton Chico to the head of Cañon Blanco, passed through the canyon, skirted along the base of the Sandia Mountains through Tijeras Canyon to the Rio Grande. Not only was water scarce and sometimes as much as half a mile off the road, but often wood and grass were hard to come by. Franz Huning, *Trader on the Santa Fe Trail*, pp. 75–81.

24. John E. Coleman was a native of Louisville, Kentucky, born in 1829. During the gold rush of 1849 he went to California where he spent fourteen years mining and prospecting before returning to his home. After a few years Coleman moved to Kansas. In 1871 he organized the group of men from Topeka who joined the prospecting party at Kit Carson. Soon after coming to Grant County, Coleman discovered gold placers on San Domingo Creek, about three miles east of Silver City. He homesteaded a section of land in this area and was successful in raising grain and vegetables by dry farming. Coleman was given the nickname "Turquoise John" after discovering the first turquoise mine in the Burro Mountains in 1875. This claim, later developed by the Occidental and Oriental Turquoise Mining Company, produced fine gem-quality stones. He also was one of the original discoverers of silver in the Mogollon Mountains. He engaged in freighting, hauling ore from the mines to the mills in Silver City, and in 1887 he laid out a wagon road from Silver City to Clifton, Arizona, via Mangas Valley, Burro Springs, and the Gila River. John Coleman died at his San Domingo Ranch in 1906 at the age of seventy-seven. *Silver City Enterprise,* October 5, 1906.

25. Edward Seymour Stone, of Stony Gate, Kingston, Leicestershire, England, listed his occupation as "gentleman." He was a partner of Robbin and Cole in locating mining claims in Grant County and probably left the area with them. *Grant County Deed Records,* Book 18, pp. 742–57. A. Lee Campbell found gambling more profitable than mining. While in Silver City he worked as banker and dealer at various saloons and gambling halls. In 1879 an irate customer put an end to his career with a six-shooter at Norton's saloon in Mesilla. Campbell was from a prominent family of Bloomington, Indiana, with a brother at Topeka, Kansas, where he probably joined the prospecting expedition. *Grant County Herald,* April 26; May 31, 1879.

26. Inventory of supplies and equipment on hand at this time as listed in Ailman's diary:

Blacksmith tools	$ 75	41 bars soap	beans
7 yoke of oxen	$610	2,750 pounds flour	pepper
2 wagons	$250	5 gallons syrup	mustard
8 ox yokes	$ 20	27 boxes baking powder	
11 pair bows	$ 11.50	1 box candles	
2 wagon covers	$ 16	1 package matches	
ox shoes and nails		25 pounds dried apples	

2 whips	4 sacks salt
6 cans axle grease	261 pounds coffee
2 water kegs	coffee mill
mining tools	16½ pounds tea
1 keg rifle powder	46½ pounds rice
1 keg blasting powder	677 pounds bacon
6 ox chains	259 pounds sugar
2 cans coal oil	5 gallons vinegar
1 coil rope	2 boxes (80 pounds) crackers

27. Travelers from the East were seldom impressed with their first sight of Albuquerque. It was described as "resembling a brickyard as seen from a distance," and "a straggling collection of adobe houses scattered amongst innumerable acequias or irrigation ditches, in the perfectly flat lowlands of the Rio Grande valley." William A. Bell, *New Tracks in North America,* pp. 239–40. In spite of its insignificant appearance, Albuquerque, founded in 1706, had long been a town of considerable importance in the territory, second only to Santa Fe. Located along the main route from Chihuahua to Santa Fe, Albuquerque was a center of trade, religion, and culture during the Spanish period, and an important military post during Mexican and early Territorial times. In 1871 it was the supply center for prosperous farms and ranches in the fertile valley of the Rio Grande.

28. The settlement of El Rito by Joaquin Mariano Pino in 1815 was an encroachment on lands used for many years by Indians from the Laguna Pueblo. The village was deserted about 1846, largely because of almost constant Navajo raids. Myra Ellen Jenkins, "The Baltasar Baca 'Grant,' History of an Encroachment," *El Palacio,* vol. 68 (1961):57–58.

29. Laguna was settled between 1689 and 1697 by Indians from neighboring pueblos. In 1699, by order of Pedro Rodriguez Cubero, governor of New Mexico, the village was officially declared the Pueblo of San José de Laguna, so named because of a large pond nearby. The pueblo was situated on a high rocky bluff on the north side of the Rio San Juan. The houses, two and three stories high, were built of sandstone and adobe. Charles H. Lange and Carroll L. Riley, ed. *The Southwestern Journals of Adolph F. Bandelier 1880–1882,* p. 278; *1883–1884,* pp. 27–29.

30. The Cubero area was cultivated at times by both Acoma and Laguna Indians, and occasionally occupied by peaceful Navajos. In 1832

men from Albuquerque purchased land from Francisco Baca, a Navajo, and established the Mexican settlement of Cubero. Jenkins, "The Baltasar Baca 'Grant,' " p. 57; n. 39.

31.   Matthew McCarty established a ranch on Acoma Indian lands around 1864. He is said to have worked as a contractor on the railroad as it was built through this area, and a railroad station on his ranch was named McCarty's. This is now a farming community of the Acoma Indians known as Santa Maria de Acoma. Lange and Riley, *Southwestern Journals, 1883–84* p. 380, n. 178.

32.   Acoma was in existence long before the Spaniards came to New Mexico and is considered the oldest continually inhabited village in the United States. The Pueblo was built on the top of a red sandstone butte some 357 feet high. The two parties probably met near the foot of the mesa rather than at the pueblo on top.

Chapter 3

1.   It was not possible to trace the exact route of the prospecting party through this stage of their journey because of the lack of landmarks and directions. It is doubtful, however, that they ever reached the vicinity of the Little Colorado River. Later developments in the story indicate that they were now on a tributary of the Tularosa River which flows into the San Francisco River near present-day Reserve, New Mexico.

2.   In 1871 there was a well established trail leading from Pinos Altos to the Gila River, up Duck Creek valley, across Cactus Flats, and down to the San Francisco River near the 'Frisco Hot Springs. *The Borderer,* June 18, 1872.

3.   Fort West was located on a high bluff overlooking the Gila River near present-day Cliff, New Mexico. The fort was established in February 1863, as a base of operations from which to wage war against the Apaches. Three companies of the First Cavalry and one company of the First Infantry, California Volunteers, garrisoned the post. The location proved unsatisfactory, and the fort was abandoned in January 1864. Although the commanding officer Capt. James H. Whitlock described Fort West as "the finest set of company quarters and headquarters buildings in the territory," it was never more than a temporary establishment. The Apaches are thought to have burned the buildings after the military abandoned the fort. Lee Myers, "Military Establishments

in Southwestern New Mexico," *New Mexico Historical Review,* Vol. 43 (1968):21–25.

4. In the spring of 1871, the new mining camp of Silver City and the small neighboring settlements suffered frequent Apache raids. Following a visit to southwestern New Mexico in May 1871, Governor Pile reported as follows: "Depredations are almost daily occurrences. Citizens cannot go from one settlement to another, although but a few miles apart, without danger of being waylaid and shot down by these savages. . . . Travel and business are almost suspended, mining operations are broken up, and that whole section of the country is in a most deplorable condition." *The Weekly New Mexican,* May 23, 1871.

5. Methods used by the federal government in dealing with the Indian problem were severely criticized by citizens of southern New Mexico and Arizona. In 1871 some twelve hundred Apaches, expressing a desire for peace, had settled on a reservation at Cañada Alamosa on the east side of the Black Range, and several hundred more were living near Camp Apache in the White Mountains of Arizona. As wards of the government, the Indians were fed and clothed. When rations were short, small bands would leave the reservation and steal what they could from the surrounding countryside. Upon returning to their government sanctuary, they were protected from any retaliation sought by pursuing civilian militia. Vincent Colyer, *Peace With the Apaches of New Mexico and Arizona.*

6. John Kidder Houston was a native of Belfast, Maine, born May 22, 1831. His family soon moved to Ohio, then to Illinois where they settled on a farm near Delavan. After completing his education at Wabash College, Indiana, he returned to Illinois where he taught school for a year. In the spring of 1853, Houston and a partner drove a herd of cattle to the gold fields of California where he went into business at Placerville. When the Civil War broke out in 1861, he was among the first to enlist. He joined Company F, Fifth California Infantry as a private, was rapidly promoted to the rank of first lieutenant, and became quartermaster of the regiment. Houston accompanied the California Volunteers to New Mexico in 1862, and four years later declined a commission in the regular army to return to civilian life. In 1866 he came to Pinos Altos where he formed a partnership with William B. Thomas, who also came to New Mexico with the California Column. Houston and Thomas located several valuable gold mines and homesteaded land near the confluence of Bear Creek and Big Cherry Creek. They established a

ranch and are said to have planted the first apple orchard in Grant County. Houston was active in politics, serving as the first probate judge when Grant County was created in 1868, and was elected to the 23rd New Mexico Territorial Legislature 1878–79. The thirty year partnership of Houston and Thomas was terminated by the death of William Thomas in December 1899. Houston died August 21, 1908, at the age of seventy-six. *Silver City Enterprise,* December 8, 1899; *Silver City Independent,* August 25, 1908.

7. Gold was discovered at Pinos Altos in May 1860. By October there were over five hundred men at work panning the gulches and searching for quartz lodes in the surrounding mountains. At the outbreak of the Civil War, many of the miners left to join the battle. The hostile Apaches seized this opportunity to drive out those who remained. After the war Pinos Altos again became active, but it never achieved the fame and prosperity that the first discoveries seemed to promise. The placers were soon worked out, water was scarce, and little capital was available for the machinery needed in lode mining and milling on a large scale. By 1871 many of the gold miners had deserted Pinos Altos for the new silver mines at Ralston and Silver City.

8. Fort Bayard was established August 21, 1866, to control the Apaches and protect miners and prospectors coming into the area to relocate mines abandoned during the Civil War and search for new claims. It was named in honor of Capt. George D. Bayard, 4th Cavalry, Brigadier General of Volunteers, who died from wounds received in the battle of Fredericksburg, 1862. A soldier arriving at Fort Bayard in July 1871, soon after Ailman was there, described the post as a desolate looking place with flat-roofed, one-story adobe buildings and log huts scattered around in an irregular square. He considered this isolated post "the final 'jumping off place' sure enough." Frank D. Reeve, ed., "Frederick E. Phelps: A Soldier's Memoirs," *New Mexico Historical Review,* Vol. 25 (1950):49–51.

9. Fort Cummings, established October 2, 1863, was located near Cooke's Spring, a watering hole on the southern route to California. Troops stationed here furnished escort to emigrants, freight trains, and stage coaches traveling through this dangerous section of Apache country. The fort was abandoned in 1873, but reoccupied during the Apache wars of the 1880's. Myers, "Military Establishments in Southwestern New Mexico," pp. 29–35.

10. The Santa Rita copper mines were first located in 1801 by Lt.

Col. Jose Manuel Carrasco, retired officer of the Spanish colonial army. Development of the vast copper deposits was done under the most adverse conditions. Santa Rita was located in the midst of hostile Apache country, one hundred fifty miles from Spanish settlements. The rich native copper, found in great abundance, was picked out with crude tools, packed on mules, and hauled over rough terrain to Chihuahua City. In spite of the difficulties, it was reported in 1807 that the copper mines were producing 20,000 mule-loads of copper annually. (Donald Jackson, ed., *The Journals of Zebulon Montgomery Pike*, Vol. 2, pp. 47–48.) Over the years the mines passed through many hands, often worked under lease from the owners. Work was frequently abandoned for long periods due to the hostility of the Apaches or because operations were not profitable enough, with the primitive methods of mining and refining used at that time, to pay the high cost of transportation. T. A. Rickard, "The Chino Enterprise," *Engineering and Mining Journal*, Vol. 116, (1923):753–58.

11.   The Mimbres River, named by the Spaniards for a certain type of willow found growing on its banks, heads in the Black Range. It flows south, disappearing and reappearing until it empties into the Laguna de Guzman, a small lake in Chihuahua, Mexico, which has no communication with the sea. From the time Spaniards began developing the Santa Rita mines, efforts were made to farm in the fertile Mimbres Valley. The hostility of the Apaches prevented establishment of any permanent settlement. After the discovery of gold at Pinos Altos in 1860, several unsuccessful attempts were made to take up farming and ranching along the Mimbres. In 1869 a party of Mexicans, disappointed in their luck at the gold mines, located on the east side of the upper river at the site of the present town of San Lorenzo. By 1871 others had taken up *ranchos* along the river, large tracts of land were under cultivation, and herds of horses and cattle grazed on the lush pasturelands. *Mining Life*, January 24, 1874.

12.   The trail across the Black Range was well known in the 1820s when it was used by fur trappers as a route to the beaver grounds of the Gila River. From the Mimbres Valley the trail followed Gavilan Creek and Dry Gavilan across the mountains via Parks Pass and along Pollock's Creek into the Berenda Valley. The trail struck the Rio Grande near present-day Truth or Consequences. George Ruhlen, "Kearney's Route From the Rio Grande to the Gila River," *New Mexico Historical Review*, Vol. 32 (1957):213–30.

13.   Las Palomas, seven miles south of Truth or Consequences, was first settled by the Garcia and Tafoya families. Hot springs located here were known for their curative powers during the Spanish and Mexican periods, and the village became a health resort in the late 1880s. Las Palomas (the doves) derived its name from the multitude of doves that nested in the cottonwoods along the river and near the springs. T. M. Pearce, *New Mexico Place Names*, p. 85.

14.   Fort McRae, located about three miles east of the Rio Grande and five miles west of the Jornada del Muerto, was established April 1863. It was one of a chain of military posts intended to protect travelers and stop Indian depredations in the general area. It was built and garrisoned by troops of the California Volunteers and named in honor of Capt. Alexander McRae, who was killed at the battle of Valverde. The post was abandoned, October 1876, except for a small detachment left behind to dispose of military property. Robert W. Frazer, *Forts of the West*, p. 100.

15.   The building of Fort Craig began in the spring of 1853. In April of the following year it was occupied by troops from abandoned Fort Conrad, nine miles to the north. The flat-roofed adobe buildings, surrounded by a high wall, were situated on a bluff overlooking the Rio Grande about thirty-four miles south of Socorro. It was near the north end of the Jornada de Muerto, a ninety mile stretch of desolate, waterless country made even more dangerous by roving bands of Apaches. Fort Craig was deactivated in the summer of 1878, when the Apaches were thought to be under control. It was reoccupied during the last campaign against the Indians, 1880–1884. Marion C. Grinstead, *Life and Death of a Frontier Fort*.

16.   Silver was discovered in the Magdalena Mountains in the spring of 1866. Early attempts to smelt the ore in crude furnaces were unsuccessful because the ore was too low grade to pay for the high transportation costs. Rossiter W. Raymond, *Statistics of Mines and Mining in the States and Territories West of the Rocky Mountains* (1870), pp. 413–14.

17.   San Marcial was founded around 1854 on the east bank of the Rio Grande thirty miles south of Socorro. It was supported by trade from nearby Fort Craig. In 1866, when the flooding river destroyed the little Mexican village, its inhabitants moved to the higher west bank. In 1871 San Marcial was only a small village consisting of a few adobe houses, a store, and the stage station. With the coming of the railroad in 1880, San Marcial became a thriving community. It was a division point on

the railroad between Albuquerque and El Paso, with a large roundhouse and repair shops. In 1929 San Marcial was completely destroyed when the Rio Grande flooded its banks in August, to be followed within a few weeks by a second flood which damaged the town beyond repair. Lenore Dils, *Horny Toad Man*, pp. 20–21, 170,

18. Numerous Mexican villages were scattered along both sides of the Rio Grande from Fort Craig to Albuquerque. Many were built on or near the sites of ancient Piro pueblos. Luis Lopez, five miles below Socorro, was named for the man who once owned the land and had a hacienda in the area. Socorro was a Spanish land grant given to several families in 1816 to encourage permanent settlement in this fertile section of the valley. Parida (Rancho de la Parida) was located across the river just above Socorro, with Lemitar a few miles to the north. Polvadera (dusty place) was ten miles above Socorro. T. M. Pearce, *New Mexico Place Names; also New Mexico, a Guide to the Colorful State*, pp. 251–53.

19. San Jose, thirty miles southwest of Albuquerque, was named for the river nearby. When the Santa Fe Railroad located a stop here in 1902, the name was changed to Suwanee. In 1914 a post office was established here to serve an area of many square miles, and the name became Correo (mail). Pearce, *New Mexico Place Names*, p. 161.

20. Around 1864 Dumas Provencher and other members of his family settled at Blue Water, in the Grants, New Mexico, area where he became a prominent lumber dealer and sawmiill operator. He served as captain in the New Mexico Volunteer Militia during the Navajo campaign of the 1880s and was active in civic and political affairs. Provencher was shot and killed November 7, 1883, while acting as an election judge at San Rafael. Lange and Riley, *Bandelier 1883–1884*, p. 308, n. 180.

21. Solomon Barth, a native of Prussia, came to America in 1855. After spending several years in California, he moved to Arizona where he worked as a freighter, storekeeper, and mail contractor. In 1866 he established a store at Cubero. He later returned to Arizona and is said to have been the founder of St. Johns, locating there when he got a contract to supply hay and grain to Fort Apache. Barth became a prominent citizen of Arizona, serving in the 11th Arizona Territorial assembly of 1880–82. Floyd S. Fierman, ed., "Nathan Bibo's Reminiscences of Early New Mexico," *El Palacio*, 68:249; Lange and Riley, *Bandelier 1883–1884*, p. 75.

22. Only a pack trail traversed the rough terrain on the west side of the Rio Grande until 1844 when Capt. Philip St. George Cooke se-

lected this route for a wagon road to California. Many emigrant trains followed Cooke's route to the California gold fields. After crossing the Mimbres River, the Silver City road left the main route and went north-west past the Hot Springs and Apache Tejo ranches to Central City, Fort Bayard, and Silver City.

Chapter 4

1. In 1869 a group of miners from Pinos Altos began farming in a small marshy valley known as *La Cienega de San Vicente,* nine miles south-west of Pinos Altos. The following year they discovered silver on a nearby hill. News of the discovery drew men from all over the territory. Tents, cabins, and brush shelters were scattered over the flats above the marsh, and the new mining camp was christened "Silver City." By the time Ailman arrived, there were over eighty-five substantial shingle-roofed buildings in the camp, including three stores, a saloon, a boarding house, two blacksmith shops, a livery stable, one paint store, and a shoe shop, *The Borderer,* March 16, 1871.

2. John R. Johnson, nicknamed "Adobe" from the manufacture and sale of adobe brick, was born in Virginia in 1827. He came to Pinos Altos after the Civil War and for many years was active in mining, lo-cating claims in almost every new district in Grant County. Johnson was elected to the New Mexico Territorial Legislature, 1871–72. At the time of his nomination, he was described as a "thorough-going, in-dustrious and energetic man, a gentleman in manners and deportment." In later years, however, Johnson was involved in a number of shooting incidents and was killed in a dispute over property boundaries at Hills-boro in 1884. *The Borderer,* May 18, 1871; *The Silver City Enterprise,* February 29, 1884.

3. Hugh Flynn was a gambler who was described as quarrelsome and dangerous. He was wounded by John Perry in a shooting incident in 1873, and was killed by Williiam Jordan in a gunfight four years later. *The Grant County Herald,* August 11, 1877.

4. Little is known about Conrad Shoemaker. He came here with Ailman's prospecting party, and he and Ailman located several mining claims near Silver City. Their cabin was on the south side of Broadway directly across the street from the property on which Ailman built a fine brick residence ten years later. In 1873 Shoemaker and Ailman dissolved their partnership, with Shoemaker taking the lot and cabin

and Ailman the undeveloped mining claims. Conrad Shoemaker ran a beer saloon and lunch room in Silver City for two years, and then he moved on—destination unknown. *Grant County Deed Records,* Book 1, pp. 296–97, 388.

5.   *The Borderer,* May 22, 1872, reported that Mr. Putnam, a young man recently arrived from Colorado, had been killed by Indians at Bremen's sawmill. A letter from Silver City, written by E. E. Burlingame, superintendent of the Tennessee mill, describes the Indian situation of 1872:

Our Indian troubles are again commencing, but I think there will hereafter be nothing serious. Last summer somebody was killed nearly every day (mostly prospectors who went outside the town hunting for mines), but no one has been murdered so far this season although a man came very near it yesterday. Nobody ever goes out of town for half a mile without carrying a revolver and rifle; it looks so queer to see a rifle on the shoulder of nearly every man you meet. Day before yesterday, a man and I went out to see some mines about ten miles from town, and he pointed out the different spots along the road where men had been killed - usually a rude cross and a pile of stones marks such places - and yesterday a man was chased over the same road to within a mile of town by them. They (the Indians) seldom attack two men when together, but their favorite method is to watch the road from some high bluff, and when a man comes along alone, they steal down into a bush close to the road ahead and shoot him as he comes along. They generally succeed in taking a man unawares, and never attack unless there are three or four of them to one white. Burlingame to Alice Hoffman, June 6, 1873.

6.   The post office was established at Pinos Altos October 4, 1867, with John A. Miller postmaster; the Silver City post office was established August 11, 1871, Harry C. Porter postmaster. H. D. Sheldon, "Territorial Post Offices of New Mexico," *New Mexico Historical Review,* Vol. 34 (1959): pp. 213, 221.

7.   Grant County mining records and newspapers of that period credit William D. Brown, not J. Ross Browne, with this important discovery. He is said to have picked up samples of silver ore when passing through southwestern New Mexico in 1869 as a member of a railroad survey party. On reaching San Francisco, Brown left the ore specimens at the mint to be assayed. The report was so promising that it created great excitement among California prospectors. A large party was organized to return with Brown to New Mexico where he located

the first claims in the Pyramid Mountains in February 1870. A town site was laid out and named Ralston City in honor of William C. Ralston, San Francisco banker, who is said to have organized and arranged financing for the expedition. *The New Mexican,* June 7, 1870; *Grant County Mining Deeds,* 1868–1870, pp. 291–95; *Grant County Deed Records,* Bk. 18, pp. 522–23.

8.   John and James Bullard, Henry M. Fuson, John Swisshelm, Elijah Weeks, Joseph T. Yankie, Richard Yeaman, and Andrew Hurlburt were among those who rushed to investigate the new discovery. They returned to the Cienega de San Vicente, where they had been farming. On May 27, 1870, they located the first claims, the Legal Tender and Twin Lodes 1 and 2, in the Silver Flat Mining District, on the hill behind the present Grant County courthouse. *Grant County Deed Records,* Bk. 18, pp. 144–47.

9.   In 1870 copper was discovered in the Clifton, Arizona, area by prospectors from Silver City while in pursuit of marauding Apaches. Several claims were located by Issac Stevens, James and Robert Metcalf, Charles and Baylor Shannon, James Bullard, and Joseph Yankie. The Indians were so troublesome that nothing could be done to develop these claims until 1872. At this time the Copper Mountain Mining District was formed, and the camp of Clifton was established. Charles H. Dunning, *Rock to Riches,* p. 73.

10.   A number of placer claims were located on the San Francisco River, commencing about two miles above Clifton and extending up the river several miles. In November 1880 these claims were sold to eastern capitalists who were said to have paid close to a million dollars for a five mile section on both sides of the river. Hydraulic works were installed in 1882, and the new camp was christened "Oro." *The Grant County Herald,* November 4, 1880; January 20, 1881.

11.   Juan N. Carrasco's smelter was near the creek at the lower end of Bullard Street. He operated several small adobe furnaces with blast supplied by blacksmith bellows. Up to May 1873, it was estimated that Carrasco had treated some three hundred tons of ore and produced about $200,000 in silver bullion. *Mining Life,* May 17, 1873.

12.   Harry Ailman, Conrad Shoemaker, and Ed Comerford located the Juniata Lode on August 18, 1871, in the Silver Flat Mining District. *Grant County Mining Locations,* Bk. 1, p. 115.

13.   April 22, 1872, Harry Ailman, C. Shoemaker, H. M. Fuson, Elijah Weeks, and William Irvin located the First Extension on the Grand

Duke Lode in the Chloride Flat district, one and a half miles west of Silver City. The ore found in this district, chiefly silver chloride with some native silver and argentite, was far richer than the ore of the Silver Flat district. The Chloride Flat mining district produced about $4,000,000 before silver mining declined in 1893. *Grant County Mining Locations*, Bk. 1, p. 114.

14.   Harvey H. Whitehill was born in 1837 at Bellefontaine, Ohio. He came west when twenty-one years old, spent some time at mining and prospecting in Colorado, and was sargeant-at-arms for the first Provisional Legislature of that territory. He enlisted in the U.S. Army at Fort Union during the Civil War, and upon completion of his service remained there as a grain contractor. Whitehill went to Elizabethtown in 1866, at the time of the gold strike. News of a new silver discovery led him to Silver City in the summer of 1870. In 1873 he started a dairy, and in 1885 bought a ranch on the Mimbres River and brought in the first herd of registered Hereford cattle from Texas. Whitehill served six terms as sheriff of Grant County between 1875–1882 and 1889–1890; he also was elected to the 1884–85 New Mexico Legislature. He died at Deming, New Mexico, September 7, 1906.

15.   Myers H. Casson was Silver City's first doctor. A native of Maryland, Dr. Casson came to New Mexico in 1870 and located several mining claims at Ralston. He moved to Silver City where he had little success at mining, but was well thought of as a physician. He died at the age of sixty-seven, June 17, 1891, following a lengthy illness.

16.   This incident was reported in *The Borderer*, December 6, 1872. A few years later Ailman was involved in another serious accident at his mine in Georgetown. As he failed to mention his own courageous deed in his memoirs, it is included here as reported in the *Grant County Herald*, January 12, 1878.

Mr. Ailman, in company with another person, was sinking a shaft, and Mr. Ailman was at the windlass. The weather was cold, and his hands very numb, of course. The handle slipped out of his hand and having a heavy bucket of rock about halfway up or more, the crank flew back at the rate of about a thousand feet per second, striking Mr. A. just under the eye and inflicting a terrible gash. Notwithstanding the heavy blow, sufficient to have knocked an ox off his pins, he threw himself forward and caught the crank and held it firmly, checking it in time to save the life of his companion at the bottom of the forty foot shaft where death, but for this would have been inevitable. This is what I call coming up to the scratch. If such a thing had occurred with 19 out of 20 men, the one in the shaft would certainly have been killed as it required herculean strength as well as great presence of mind to have acted as Mr. Ailman did on this occasion.

17.   In assaying for silver and gold, a sample of ore was melted with fluxes and reagents to produce a lead button containing the precious metals, and a slag which was discarded. The lead button was then melted in an oxidizing atmosphere to oxidize the lead and leave a bead of gold and silver alloy. The bead was weighed and then treated with nitric acid to dissolve the silver. The weight of the remaining gold, subtracted from total weight of the bead, gave the amount of silver contained in the ore sample.

18.   Martin W. Bremen, a man of great energy and determination, became one of the most successful mine and mill operators in Grant County. Born in New York around 1840, Bremen came to Pinos Altos, New Mexico, following the Civil War. He homesteaded a ranch and set-up a steam-operated sawmill, supplying lumber to the mining camps and military posts within a 200 mile radius. In the fall of 1871, Bremen brought an old eleven-stamp gold mill from Pinos Altos and set it up in Silver City near San Vincente Creek. Using wooden barrels for amalgamation, run by rawhide belting and an engine that had seen better days, it is said to have taken the combined efforts of every able-bodied man in camp to get the thing started. Bremen's was the first stamp mill in the new camp. Because of its worn-out condition, by June of the following year only five stamps were usable, but Bremen still managed to turn out $2,422 in refined silver in one week. Martin Bremen became one of the most prominent mining men in Grant County, steadily improving his mill and buying up valuable mining property, the most important being the "76" mine in Chloride Flat. Up to 1887, when he sold his interests to an eastern syndicate, he had produced over $2,500,000 in silver bullion. Bremen next went to Arizona where for a time he operated a gold mine near Globe, successful at first, but soon ending in failure. Broke, discouraged, and ill, on November 3, 1887, he ended his life by taking an overdose of morphine.

19.   Dan Dugan came to Colfax County, New Mexico, after the Civil War. Reports of the silver strike drew him to Silver City in September 1870. Mining in the early days was an uncertain business, and most of the prospectors had to find another way of making a living. In 1873 Dugan moved to the Gila Valley where he engaged in farming and

ranching, prospecting when he could. He gained fame in 1877 as one of the original discoverers of gold at Hillsboro in the Black Range. He also located several claims in the Kingston area and moved to a ranch near Lake Valley. When Dugan died, June 21, 1884, his estate, which included land, mines, mills, and cattle, was estimated to be worth $150,000. *Southwest Sentinel,* June 28, 1884. Ailman attached the following footnote to his memoirs:

In 1874 a roving photographer named Brown was in the area making pictures. One day Dugan met him as both were in the act of crossing the Gila River. What the trouble was, I do not know, but Dan pulled his gun, fired, and Brown tumbled into the river. At the trial Dugan's council claimed the man drowned. The jury seemed to accept that idea, and Dan escaped the hangman's noose.

The shooting occurred November 20, 1874. Dugan was tried at Las Cruces in June of the following year. After three days of deliberation, the jury found him not guilty. *Mining Life,* November 21, 1874; *Grant County Herald,* June 27, 1875.

20. A process called "barrel amalgamation" was used in these early attempts to produce silver bullion. The ore was first crushed in a large grinding pit, called an *arastra,* or by stamp mill. It was then dumped into wooden barrels and water, quicksilver, salts, and various chemicals were added. As the barrels were rotated, the water carried off the lighter materials while the amalgamated metal sank to the bottom. The mercury was burned off and the remaining silver molded into bars. During the week ending June 22, 1872, $4,790 in silver bullion was produced in Silver City by amalgamation and $2,200 in silver extracted by adobe furnaces. Rossiter W. Raymond, *Statistics of Mines and Mining,* 1873, p. 310.

21. David Winterburn, a native of England, came to Grant County in 1867. He spent the next ten years in prospecting and mining with only moderate success. In 1878 he finally made a rich discovery near Georgetown. He located the Silver Queen mine, sold it for a good price, and left the country.

22. Dr. Rollin C. Anderson, from Aurora, Illinois, was no stranger to southwestern New Mexico. In Missouri, in the latter part of 1866, he organized the American and Gila River Mining and Agricultural Association for the purpose of colonizing and developing the Gila Valley. They got as far as Pinos Altos but were not able to proceed with their plan until the spring of 1868. At that time twenty-four families moved

to the Gila and selected land not far from the abandoned site of Fort West. They cleared and planted the land, but they found themselves in constant danger from marauding Apaches who ran off all the stock and finally forced the settlers to abandon the project. *The New Mexican,* March 17, 1868; *Mogollon Mines,* 1913, p. 40.

23. In the fall of 1872 Dr. Anderson sent Professor James Fish, a geologist from Chicago, to make an extensive prospecting tour of New Mexico. Professor Fish reported finding the richest ores at Silver City and purchased a number of claims there in February 1873. In the meantime, Anderson organized the New Mexico Silver Mining Company of Chicago, a colony of over sixty people, including wives and children. Early in May they set out for New Mexico, traveling by train as far as the end of the railroad. They brought eight railroad carloads of baggage and supplies, plus horses and wagons in which to complete the journey. The colony arrived in Silver City in mid-July 1873. *Mining Life,* May 31, July 26, 1873.

24. The New Mexico Silver Mining Company of Chicago failed in a very short time. By August 1873, when the milling machinery and equipment reached Silver City, the company was already in financial trouble. They mortgaged the machinery and were unable to redeem it. A lien was put on their mill site, and the machinery was sold to satisfy creditors. *Grant County Deed Book 1,* pp. 524, 567; *Deed Book 2,* pp. 14–17.

25. Robert Florman was a native of Prussia. In 1862 he was in Denver, Colorado, operating Florman's Confectionery and Ice Cream Saloon on Larimer Street. He spent several years prospecting and mining in Colorado and Montana, and by 1870 was in the confectionery business at Elizabethtown, New Mexico. The following year he came to Silver City where he invested in real estate and mining property, selling out in 1875 to go prospecting in the gold fields of South Dakota. In 1885 the *Pierre* (South Dakota) *Signal* reported that Florman had been the first to discover silver in the Black Hills, in 1877, and had made several fortunes and lost them again in other mining ventures. He and his family were living in Rapid City where he was investing his latest fortune in cattle and real estate. *Southwest Sentinel,* February 21, 1885.

26. The Chino copper mine was located in July 1872 by James Fresh and John Magruder. This started a flurry of activity in the area, with several claims and relocations made on the old Santa Rita del Cobre property. In September 1873, the Santa Rita mining district was organ-

ized by Harry Ailman, David Winterburn, Robert Florman, Dan Dugan, A. Robins, G. B. McCampbell, Joseph Williams, and W. H. Wray. *The Tribune,* September 5, 1873; *Grant County Mine Locaitons,* Book 1, pp. 62–68, 132.

27.   James Fresh came to Grant County in 1869 as mine superinten-dent for Sweet and LaCosta of San Antonia, Texas, who held a lease on the Santa Rita copper mine. In 1871 mining was discontinued at Santa Rita because the methods used to smelt the copper were unprof-itable. In July 1872, Fresh and John R. Magruder, who had recently arrived from Washington, D.C., formed a partnership to develop the Chino copper mine. The copper was smelted in an old adobe furnace at the San Jose mine, also owned by Fresh and Magruder.

28.   The eastern side of the Parapet Mountains, northeast of Santa Rita, was prospected in 1872 by J. W. Read, who pronounced the ore too low-grade to pay for mining and milling. James Fresh had a different opinion. On May 5, 1873, he located fourteen mining claims and a mill site in this area which later became Georgetown. *Mining Life,* July 26, 1873; *Mine Locations,* Book 1, pp. 133–40.

Chapter 5

1.   The Mimbres Mining District was organized in July 1873, but the new mining camp did not receive the name Georgetown until late the following year. There were several reasons for selecting this name. John Magruder, partner of James Fresh in locating the first claims in the new district, was from Georgetown in the District of Columbia. Stan-ton Brannin, also one of the first to locate claims in the new mining district, was a native of Georgetown, Wisconsin. Several others who were living in the new camp had come from Colorado where George-town was the site of the first important silver discovery of that state. They felt that the ore of the Mimbres Mining District compared favora-bly with that of Colorado and therefore named the new camp George-town after the Colorado camp. *Mining LIfe,* July 17, 1873; *Grant County Herald,* January 2, 1875.

2.   Hartford M. (Henry) Meredith was an experienced prospector who had been in the mining game for many years. He was born July 9, 1840, at Litchfield, Kentucky, attended school there, and at the age of thirteen left home to support himself. He served with distinction dur-ing the Civil War, raising his own troop of Kentucky Cavalry, of which

he was captain until mustered out of the service in 1864. Meredith then went to Montana where he spent several years prospecting in the vicinity of Helena. In 1867 he joined the rush to a promising new silver discovery in the White Pine mining district of eastern Nevada. This was a short-lived boom, and by 1869 he was prospecting in California. Early the following year, hearing rumors of a silver strike in southwestern New Mexico, he came to try his luck at a place called Ralston. After locating a few claims, he sold out and moved on to another new discovery at Silver City. By the time he joined forces with Harry Ailman at Georgetown, Meredith had prospected many areas of Grant County with little success. *An Illustrated History of Skagit and Snohomish Counties*, pp. 1098–99.

    3.   The most valuable ore in the Georgetown area was cerargyrite (horn silver). It occurred in Fusselman limestone, often in blanket-like deposits along or near dikes directly below the dark Percha shale. Small amounts of native silver, argentite, and galena were also present. S. G. Lasky and T. P. Wooton, *The Metal Resources of New Mexico and Their Economic Features*, p. 67.

    4.   Mining laws enacted May 10, 1872, stated that no location of a mining claim could be made until the vein or lode was discovered within the claim. The discoverer must first sink a shaft upon the lode to a depth of at least ten feet to show mineral bearing rock. He must then post a notice at the point of discovery showing name of lode, locator, and date of discovery, and mark the surface boundaries. Claims could not exceed fifteen hundred feet in length and six hundred feet in width. R. S. Morrison, *Mining Rights in the Western States and Territories*, pp. 17–23.

    5.   Elijah Weeks was considered one of the best judges of ore in Grant County. He was born at Greasy Creek, Patrick County, Virginia, in 1835. He was in the mining business for several years in North Carolina and Missouri before coming to Pinos Altos, New Mexico, in 1869. The following year, Weeks and his associates discovered silver on Legal Tender Hill and filed the first mining claim in the Silver City area. In 1874 he moved to Georgetown and worked for Fresh and Magruder until the latter part of 1879 when he returned to Silver City to promote the development of the Legal Tender mine as vice-president of the New Mexico and Massachusetts Mining Company. He supervised construction of the mill, but died of pneumonia in April 1880, before seeing it in operation. *Grant County Herald*, April 10, 1880.

    6.   Meredith and Ailman began work on their claim June 15, 1874.

Their discovery was announced in the *Grant County Herald,* November 14, 1874, as follows: "Harry Ailman and Henry Meredith have made a big strike on the 1st extension southeast of the Piute in the Mimbres District. Their shaft is about sixty feet deep. The vein lies between the granite and lower lying shale. The boys deserve their good luck as they have worked hard all summer."

7.   The average market value of silver in 1872 was $1.32 per fine ounce. (Fine ounce means containing a specified proportion of pure metal per ounce.) The Fourth Coinage Act, passed February 12, 1873, stopped the minting of the standard silver dollar, although a heavier silver dollar was still produced for foreign trade. This dropped the price of silver to $1.28 per ounce by 1874. Increased production of silver from new discoveries in the West and the adoption of the gold standard by Germany, Holland and Scandinavia (1875) brought a further decline in the market. In June of 1876, Silver City merchant-banker H. M. Porter announced that "owing to the depreciation in value of silver in Eastern markets," he could pay only 95¢ per ounce. The following month the price dropped to 90¢ per ounce. *Grant County Herald,* June 24, 1876 and July 15, 1876.

8.   The Bland-Allison Act, February 28, 1878, authorized the secretary of the treasury to purchase not less than two million and not more than four million dollars worth of silver per month to be used for silver dollars. This measure did little to stop the steady decline in the price of silver. Richard B. Morris, *Encyclopedia of American History,* p. 254.

9.   The Mimbres Reduction Works began operation August 1874. Magruder handled the mill work, and Fresh was in charge of the Georgetown mines and the Chino copper property. The reduction works consisted of two adobe furnaces capable of turning out two thousand pounds of copper per day, a cupola and refining furnace which could produce fifteen hundred ounces of silver a week, and arastras for crushing the ore. In May 1876, a stamp mill and Frue concentrator were added to greatly increase production. *Grant County Herald,* November 21, 1875; May 15, 1876.

10.   Jerome Ailman was born on a farm in Juniata County, Pennsylvania, October 5, 1849. After attending school until the age of sixteen, he obtained his first teaching job at Denholm, in adjacent Mifflin County. In the years that followed, Jerome taught in various country schools to earn money for the advancement of his own education. After graduating from Princeton University in 1877, he accepted a teaching position

in Texas, but after two terms he returned to Pennsylvania where he became principal of Airy View Academy at Perrysville. Biographical information from family records courtesy of Mildred A. Ailman. See also Chapter 6, n. 25.

11.   Commodore Perry Crawford was born near East Liverpool, Ohio, in 1845. He served with the Ohio Volunteer Infantry during the Civil War. After the war, he came west to try his luck in the Colorado gold fields. By 1870 new mining discoveries had led him to Elizabethtown, New Mexico, where he met Henry M. Porter, a prosperous merchant. Porter sent Crawford to Silver City, in the fall of 1873, to take charge of his general mercantile business. C. P. Crawford was an enterprising young man, and this was just what the new mining camp needed. Within a short time, he had built up a thriving wholesale and retail business and opened a bank in connection with the store. He handled Porter's mining interests in southern New Mexico and Arizona, and never missed an opportunity to promote the Grant County area. In 1880 Crawford became a partner of Porter in the Silver City business, and two years later he bought out Porter's interest. He began construction of an imposing brick building on the corner of Bullard and Broadway to house his store and bank, and invested heavily in the mines in various parts of the southwest. In December 1883 the Crawford bank failed and he lost everything. Crawford continued with mining interests for the rest of his life in an effort to recoup his losses. He was killed by falling down a shaft at his mine in Santa Rita, August 23, 1907. Crawford was a generous, public spirited man, highly regarded in the Southwest. Probably no one person was more responsible for the building up of Silver City and the surrounding camps than C. P. Crawford.

12.   In 1871 Lucien B. Maxwell, owner of the Maxwell Land Grant in northern New Mexico, purchased machinery for a stamp mill that he intended erecting at Silver City. The machinery had reached Fort Cummings when Maxwell received a discouraging report on the new silver mines. He decided to abandon the project and left the machinery at the fort. Early in 1873 Valentine S. Shelby of Santa Fe, purchased the mill from Maxwell and brought it to Silver City. The Tennessee Reduction Company was organized by Shelby, H. M. Porter of Cimarron, and local investors Isaac J. Stevens, Thomas Lyons, Isaac Givens, and Richard Hudson. Eugene E. Burlingame, territorial assayer of Colorado, was hired to superintend the operation. A building was erected, the machinery installed, and in May the mill was ready for business. Within a few

months, however, it was decided that roasters were needed to reduce the ores of this area profitably. In order to make these improvements, the company mortgaged the mill to H. M. Porter. Unfortunately, the new equipment did not increase production as expected, and the company was unable to pay off the note. Porter took over, putting his manager, C. P Crawford in charge of the mill until 1877 when it was sold to Martin Bremen. *Mining Life*, March 28, 1874.

13.   James A. Lucas was born in Boonville, Missouri, June 5, 1826. He came to El Paso, Texas with the U.S. Army during the war with Mexico and remained there to operate a mercantile business with his brother, John, who was U.S. Consul to Mexico. James served as vice-consul for a year, 1850–51, then moved to Mesilla, New Mexico, where he established a mercantile business. He was elected to the New Mexico Territorial Legislature in 1854, and served as probate clerk of Doña Ana County, 1854–59. Lucas was a strong Southern sympathizer during the Civil War. When Colonel Baylor invaded southern New Mexico and established the Confederate Territory of Arizona, Lucas was appointed secretary of the new government. He later followed the retreating Confederate Army to San Antonio, Texas. In 1864 he was appointed to the customs office at Eagle Pass, Texas, but he soon returned to Mesilla to operate a drug store on the plaza. In 1866 Lucas moved his family to Missouri in order to give the children a better education, returning to New Mexico in 1873 to settle on a farm in the Mimbres Valley. He operated a store and ran a grist mill on power furnished by a turbine wheel. In 1875 he attached arastras to the turbine to grind silver-bearing quartz, and the following year converted the grist mill to a stamp mill.

14.   The Lucas mill was sold to Meredith and Ailman in May of 1877 for $3,850 plus a hotel in Georgetown. Lucas ran the hotel, engaged in mining, and served as Georgetown postmaster and notary public. In 1881 he went into the cattle business with his sons, and three years later moved to Silver City where he remained until his death in 1900. *Silver City Enterprise*, November 30, 1900.

15.   The vanner operated on the same principle as the gold pan. It was a wide rubber conveyor belt set on a slant. As crushed ore was fed onto the moving belt, water flowed over it, washing away the lighter materials while the heavier particles of precious metal clung to the belt. Charles H. Dunning, *Rock to Riches*, p. 28.

16.   At the time Meredith and Ailman bought the Lucas mill, they were down 125 feet on the Naiad Queen and had struck an extremely

rich body of ore assaying as high as 2,000 ounces of silver per ton. With the installation of the overshot water wheel and new milling machinery, they were able to work even their low grade ore at a profit. *Grant County Herald,* May 26, 1877; June 29, 1878.

17.   John Spillar was considered one of the best mill men in the southwest. He was born in the state of New York around 1849, but nothing is known of his early years. He came to Pinos Altos in the late 1860s and worked at the Pacific mine. When silver was discovered at Ralston in 1870, Spillar located a claim with H. M. Meredith and others. He appears to have been more interested in the milling business than in prospecting, as his name seldom appears on the mining deed records. After Meredith and Ailman sold the Georgetown mill, Spillar continued as superintendent for the new owners until 1885. At this time he acquired an interest in the Magregor mill in Georgetown. In 1888 Spillar accepted a position with an English company in Mexico, but returned to Georgetown the following year. He became superintendent of the Pacific mine and mill at Pinos Altos in 1890, later acquiring a lease on this property which he worked until it was sold to the George Hearst estate in 1897. Evidently John Spillar left the area; no further record of his activities could be found.

18.   Samuel H. Ailman and his twin brother, Herbert I., were born at the family farm near Mexico, Pennsylvania, October 31, 1853. Like Harry and Jerome, they attended school until qualifying for a teaching certificate, then taught in the nearby schools and helped on the farm. Sam came to New Mexico in 1877 and worked at the mill until the Georgetown property was sold. He went into the ranching business with Stanton Brannin on the Sapillo River, west of the Mimbres. In 1881 brother Herbert arrived and the two boys located what was known as the Brannin Park Ranches in Rocky Canyon. They developed a fine herd of cattle and raised thoroughbred horses. In 1886 they sold their ranches and stock for $16,000 to George O. Smith, originator of the G.O.S. ranch. Herbert returned to Pennsylvania where he died in 1940. Sam remained in the West for a time, but returned to Pennsylvania around 1918 and lived there until his death in 1927. Biographical notes courtesy of Mildred A. Ailman, Oxford, Pennsylvania.

19.   Meredith and Henry Fitch went to investigate the new camp south of Cow Springs in April 1877. On their return trip they were ambushed by twenty or more Indians. Fitch was wounded in the side, the shoulder and both feet. Meredith was shot in the leg and back, and a

glancing bullet hit his arm and broke two ribs. *Grant County Herald,*
April 7, 1877.

20.   H. M. Meredith and Minnie, daughter of David and Mary Bunn,
were married at Valley Home, the Meredith residence on the Mimbres
River, April 24, 1878. As soon as news of the event reached Georgetown,
friends gathered to give the newly-weds a glorious old-time *chiravari,*
"which was received with unanimous applause by a most appreciative
audience. The solos on the triangle and powder keg were unusually fine
and literally brought down the house! The chorus of sobs by the disappointed single gentlemen was extremely well rendered. At the conclusion of the open-air concert the performers were most hospitably regaled
with refreshments by the father and mother of the bride." *Grant County
Herald,* April 27, 1878.

21.   A winch, called a whim, was used to hoist ore or water from
the mine shaft. It consisted of a vertical drum with crossarms and was
turned by a horse hitched to the crossbar.

22.   Footnote from Ailman memoirs: "Ira E. Smith, whose ancestors came to America on the Mayflower, was born in New York. As a
young man he studied for the Methodist ministry, and as an additional
safeguard he became proficient in the carpenter's trade. While serving a
church in Flint, Michigan, he met and married Nancy Cooper. Theora
Virginia was born in July 20, 1856. Finding the salary of a small country
church rather inadequate to support a family, Mr. Smith moved to Chicago where he applied his carpenter trade. He erected several large buildings for the elder Studebaker, founder of the wagon corporation, and
was offered certain city lots as part payment. As he could not see the
future of the city, he declined. He moved to Springfield, then on to St.
Louis where he accepted a position at the city water works. Mr. Smith
enlisted in the Civil War and was used as a spy. After the war he went
to Kansas City and worked in the passenger car shops. He later secured
farm land down on the Miosha River in southern Kansas, hiring the
farming done while he worked as a carpenter. After three years of
grasshoppers, fever, and ague, he decided to look elsewhere for a more
healthy location. Leaving his family on the farm, he started west. On
arriving in Silver City, he was employed by Robert Black for about a
year then returned for his family. Five neighbors decided to join him in
the wagon train to New Mexico." (See Virginia Smith Ailman's story,
Appendix A).

23.   Robert Black constructed most of the important early buildings

in Silver City. He was born March 14, 1840, at Cambridge, Massachusetts. As a young man, he learned the building trade and became proficient as an architect and draftsman. In 1871 he moved to Denver, Colorado, and the following year he came to Silver City to erect a mill building. He liked the prospects of this lively new mining camp and decided to remain here, opening a carpenter shop with his brother Thomas. In 1875 Black formed a partnership with Eugene Cosgrove to operate a lumber yard. From the east they brought machinery for the first planing mill in New Mexico. Black and Cosgrove furnished lumber as far away as Fort Bowie and Tucson, Arizona. By 1879 the firm was employing twenty-seven men, with construction superintendents in Silver City, Georgetown, Fort Bayard, Hillsboro, and Eureka. Robert Black was the first mayor of Silver City, elected in 1878, 1879, and again in 1883. He served as president of the Silver City School Board for over twenty years, and while a member of the New Mexico Legislature in 1880, introduced the first public school bill. He was elected to the Grant County Board of Commissioners, 1891–92, served for several years on the Board of Regents of the Agricultural College as Las Cruces and was a member of the first Board of Regents at the Normal School at Silver City. Robert Black died July 7, 1910, after suffering a stroke. *Silver City Enterprise,* July 8, 1910.

24.   The Gila Cliff Dwellings are located in the Gila Natonal Forest, about fifty miles north of Silver City. Archaeologists believe these pueblo-type dwellings were built around A.D. 1100 by Indians of the Mogollon culture and occupied for about 250 years. The Gila Cliff Dwellings National Monument was established November 16, 1907, to preserve these historic ruins.

25.   The mummy was discovered in 1889 by the Hill brothers who owned the Hot Springs ranch. In 1892 they conducted a representative of the Smithsonian Institution through the cliff dwellings and turned the mummy over to him. Photographs of the mummy and several other pictures in the Ailman collection were taken by Rev. R. E. Pierce, pastor of the Methodist Church in Silver City. Benjamin Pierce, *Memories of Pierces in Parsonages,* pp. 9–11.

26.   *The Grant County Herald,* August 3, 1878, commented on Ailman's wedding as follows: "The matrimonial business seems to be looking up. One of our staid old bachelors was gathered in this week. . . . It is to be regretted that Ailman don't live in Silver City. So many here,

without referring to tin pans and horse-fiddle, would be glad to congratulate him upon his exit from bachelorhood."

27. The Naiad Queen was the best paying mine in Georgetown. Each report during 1879 showed increasing returns. In July Meredith brought to Silver City seven silver bricks with a total weight of 966 pounds, worth nearly $16,000. Net profits for the month of November averaged $266 a day. By December they were down 240 feet following a vein of silver two feet wide running along the lower side of the porphyry wall. Here a single shot opened out a five-foot vein of ore and knocked out some solid chunks of metal as big as a man's head. *Grant County Herald,* December 13, 1878; June 14, 1879; December 6, 1879.

28. Harry W. Elliott came from Tennessee where several members of his family were prominent in the legal profession. He was a graduate of the University of Texas with a degree in law. He arrived in New Mexico in 1876 and was admitted to practice law in the district court of the territory in July of that year. Elliott, however, was more interested in learning the business of mining and prospecting. He was described as a tall, rawboned Tennessean, an independent character, but generous and loyal to those he liked. He was a dynamic speaker, and was often called upon to address Georgetown public gatherings. David H. Stratton, ed. *The Memoirs of Albert B. Fall,* pp. 32–33.

29. John D. Pancake, a cousin of C. P. Crawford, arrived from Blandinsville, Illinois, in July 1878. After working for Ailman for a year, he bought a ranch on the lower Gila. He spent many years prospecting in southwestern New Mexico and adjacent Arizona, probably grub-staked by Crawford.

30. Harry Elliott and Robert Forbes prospected the Stein's Peak area in the fall of 1879. Elliott located the Centipede and Not Yet lode in the Granite Peak District. *Grant County Mine Locations,* Book 1, pp. 793–94.

31. Harry Pye was born and raised in Cornwall, England. He came to Georgetown in 1875 and worked there about three years. In 1878, while prospecting on the east side of the Black Range with Gus Holmes, he located the Pye lode, the first silver discovery in the vicinity of Chloride, New Mexico. Pye returned to the claim to do the development work the following year. He and his helper were killed by Indians, November 1879, while on their way back to Hillsboro. *Grant County Herald,* October 4, 1879; December 18, 1880.

32. Harry Elliott and Robert Forbes were among the first to discover silver on Percha Creek in the Black Range in the fall of 1880. The mining camp of Kingston took its name from Elliott's mine, the Iron King, which he sold two years later for $25,000. The Brush Heap, located and developed by Elliott and Forbes, became one of the leading producers of the area, providing the partners with a large and steady income for many years. In 1883 Elliott and H. L. Pickett, a classmate from Tennessee, opened law offices in Silver City and Hillsboro. The following year Elliott was elected to the New Mexico Territorial Legislature. Before his term was up, however, he began to lose his eyesight. Leaving Forbes in charge of the Brush Heap, and Pickett to run the law practice, Elliott spent the next four years traveling all over the world seeking a cure. He returned to New Mexico only for short visits to handle important law cases, one of which was to cause a great deal of trouble for Meredith and Ailman. By 1892 Elliott had fully recovered his health and sight and was living in Boston, Massachusetts, where he was considered a very successful financier. Some years later he moved to Bellvue, Arkansas, where he died in 1925.

33. Stanton S. Brannin was born in Wisconsin in 1846. He came to Golden, New Mexico, in 1868, and two years later moved to Lincoln County where he had a contract to furnish deer and antelope meat for Fort Stanton. Hearing of the mining activities in Grant County, Brannin came to investigate and was one of the early discoverers of silver at Georgetown, locating the Satisfaction lode in May 1873. In 1878 Brannin and his family homesteaded a ranch on the Sapillo and he went into the sawmill and lumber business. In 1880 he put a manager in charge of his sawmill and devoted his energies to ranching. Brannin served on the Board of Grant County Commissioners 1893–95, then sold his ranch and moved his family to Montana. Julia Brannin Cannon, "Silver Boom Town," *New Mexico Magazine,* Vol. 29 (July 1951):23, 45, 47.

34. William J. Mallory located his claim, the Mayflower Extension, February 20, 1874. The dispute started in November, when Mallory began to develop his claim and it was found to overlap Brannin's Satisfaction lode. The case went to court and was finally settled when Brannin was granted a U.S. patent. In writing of this dispute, Brannin's daughter said, "All that litigation cost money, but friends helped. At one time bankers Meredith and Ailman loaned him $5,000 without even his signature as security." Cannon, p. 45; *Grant County Mine Locations,* Book 1, p. 197; *Grant County Deed* Book 3, p. 238.

35. Mallory sold the Mayflower to Meredith and Ailman in October of 1877 for $287, on the condition that the money would be returned if the case was not decided in his favor. When patent was granted to Brannin, Mallory skipped the country leaving behind a number of irate creditors. *Grant County Herald,* February 9, 1878; *Grant County Deed Book* 3, p. 219.

36. Meredith and Ailman sold their half-interest in the Satisfaction lode December 1877, to William B. Stevens and Edward Waters for $4,000. *Grant County Deed Book* 3, pp. 277–78.

37. Gen. George Crook was transferred from the Military Department of Arizona where he had been in command since 1871, to the Department of the Platte in 1875. Therefore, he was not in the Southwest at the time of the raid described by Ailman. No matter how able the military might have been, there were always too few troops to cover the vast areas of New Mexico and Arizona for which they were responsible. They received much criticism from the citizens who were subjected to repeated Apache depredations. *Grant County Herald,* May 26, 1877.

38. John Magruder went to Leadville, Colorado, in June 1878. He supervised the construction of a smelter for the Adelaide Consolidated Silver Mining and Smelting Company and was superintendent after the smelter was in operation. *Grant County Herald,* June 15, 1878; October 12, 1878.

39. James Duncan Hague was born in Boston, Massachusetts, February 24, 1836. He was educated at Harvard and abroad as a mining engineer. From 1867 to 1869 he served as an assistant geologist on the U.S. Geological Survey of the 40th parallel, then returned to the mining profession. *Appleton's Cyclopaedia of American Biography,* p. 26.

40. In October 1879, Magruder brought mining engineers W. D. Waldbridge and James D. Hague to examine the mines of Georgetown. *Grant County Herald,* October 12, 1879.

41. The Mimbres Mining Company was incorporated April 3, 1880, by James Hague, Thomas F. and T. Henry Mason, A. Gifford Agnew, and William Hart. Their purchase of the Naiad Queen and the Fresh and Magruder property was the first investment of outside capital in Georgetown, either for development or working of the mines. *Grant County Herald,* January 24, 1880.

42. While waiting for the company to take up their option on the Naiad Queen, Meredith and Ailman leased the mine to Ben St. Cyr

and partners. St. Cyr and Company made over $5,000 profit on the mine during the three months lease. St. Cyr purchased the Silver City-Georgetown express line from George Armstrong and put on a tri-weekly coach. In January 1881, St. Cyr sold his interest in the stage line, settled up his business affairs, and quietly and mysteriously disappeared from the Grant County scene. *The New Southwest,* January 1, 1882.

Chapter 6

1.   The Southern Pacific Railroad, building east from California, reached the junction in December 1880. Three months later the Santa Fe line was completed from the north, and a cluster of tents and wooden shanties formed the nucleus of the new railroad town of Deming, New Mexico.

2.   By 1880 Silver City was the supply center for all of the southwestern corner of New Mexico. Local merchants received over four million pounds of goods annually from the East and carried on a thriving wholesale and retail trade. They purchased gold and silver bullion from the surrounding mining camps and sent it to the East. Before the Southern Pacific Railroad was completed, copper from the mines at Clifton, Arizona, was shipped through Silver City. There were sixty-eight farms under cultivation in the Mimbres and Gila valleys, and sheep and cattle ranches were beginning to take over the productive grazing lands.

3.   Reynolds and Griggs, long established mercants of Mesilla, New Mexico, opened a branch store in Silver City in 1872, with A. H. Morehead as manager. In 1877 Joseph Reynolds moved to Silver City to carry on the business. When Meredith and Ailman took over the Reynolds store, it was located in a large one-story brick building, 35 feet by 150 feet, on the northwest corner of Bullard and Broadway, with a smaller commercial wareroom adjoining the stores on the north. They remodeled the premises, adding a second story and an impressive dark green iron front with plate glass windows lettered in gilt.

4.   Isaac James Stevens (1811–85) was a farmer from Maine who came west in 1859. After a year in Colorado where his family joined him, he moved to the Maxwell Land Grant in northern New Mexico. For several years he prospered as a farmer and road builder, then moved the family to a farm north of Denver in order to provide schooling for his children. In 1870 Stevens came to Silver City, decided the new mining camp had a future, and moved his family to Grant County. Stevens

and his oldest son, Isaac N., engaged in mining and real estate, locating several claims which later proved to be good producers. He purchased farm land south of town and raised vegetables for local consumption. In 1878 the Stevens family move to Clifton, Arizona, where Isaac and his sons, Ike, Charlie, and Albert located some of the best mines in that region. He died at Clifton in August 1885 at the age of 74. He was buried at Clifton, but five years later his body was brought to Silver City and laid to rest in the Masonic cemetery. Marie Stevens Milliken, *Isaac James Stevens, His Experience As a Pioneer.*

5. The Meredith and Ailman houses were among the first of a number of elegant Victorian homes erected in Silver City during the prosperous 1880s. They were identical one-and-a-half story Mansard-roofed brick houses with two-and-a-half story dormered cupolas. Plans for the houses apparently were taken from A. J. Bicknell's *Detail, Cottage and Constructive Architecture,* a popular builder's guide published in 1873. The houses stood on the north side of Broadway between Arizona and Pinos Altos streets. In 1905 the Meredith house was torn down and reassembled at another location a few blocks away; it was later remodeled beyond recognition. The Ailman house passed through several hands, serving as a boarding house for some twenty years prior to 1926, when it was purchased by the Town of Silver City. The building was first used as a City Hall, and after 1931 it became the fire station. Today it is the home of the Silver City Museum. Susan Berry, *Survey of Historic Buildings in Silver City,* 1979.

6. In the fall of 1882, Meredith and Ailman employed Tom Carson and China Joe at $35 per month, Charley Rosencranz at $100 monthly, and John M. Smith at $125 per month. In October they hired West Welty to work for three months at $85 a month plus goods for himself and family at cost, on the condition that he would leave whiskey and cards alone. *Ailman Memorandum Book.*

7. In 1857 Lawrence P. Browne joined Kansas City merchant, Washington H. Chick in the business of overland freighting to the Southwest. As the railroad built across the plains, Chick, Browne & Co. followed, establishing stores at Leavenworth, Junction City, Ellsworth, and Sheridan, Kansas, and at Kit Carson and Granada, Colorado. From there they followed the construction of the Santa Fe Railroad into New Mexico, making their headquarters at Las Vegas. Francisco A. Manzanares, a native New Mexican of Spanish ancestry, became a member of the firm after attending school in St. Louis and New York.

When Chick retired from the business, the firm became Browne, Manzanares & Co. After the railroad reached Socorro, Browne and Manzanares built a branch store there. Acting as agents for merchants throughout the southwest, they accepted goods from eastern markets, paid freight charges, and arranged for transportaton by wagon to destination. They were paid a commission for their services and also carried on a flourishing wholesale business in staples. Ralph Emerson Twitchell, *Leading Facts of New Mexican History*, pp. 448–49.

8.   The employing of friendly Apache as scouts was originated by Lt. Howard B. Cushing while he was stationed in Arizona 1869–71. When Gen. George Crook took command of the Military Department of Arizona, July 1871, he established the first company of scouts at Camp Apache. Martin F. Schmitt, *General George Crook*, p. 166.

9.   A similar incident was reported in the *Southwest Sentinel,* March 10, 1883, as follows:

Two years ago a company of Apache scouts, having received three months back pay, invested their money in Silver City, and among the articles purchased were clean white glossy shirts. Several wore them outside their black cashmere vests, enjoying their new dress amazingly. Others sported their clean linen having nothing else to cover their nakedness except a breechclout and a pair of moccasins.

10.   Trade with Mexico amounted to several hundred thousand dollars annually. Silver City merchants made a neat profit by exchanging manufactured goods for silver dollars which contained more silver than U.S. dollars. Maize, frijoles, corn, flour, sugar, oranges, lemons, cheese and candy were also brought in from south of the border.

11.   November 24, 1883, Kit Joy, A. M. (Mitch) Lee, Frank Taggart, and George Cleveland held up the train five miles east of Gage Station. They shot the engineer and took between seven and eight hundred dollars. By the end of January all four men had been captured and jailed in Silver City to await trial. *The Enterprise*, January 4, 11, 15, 1884.

12.   J. C. Jackson, a popular and enterprising merchant, came to Silver City from Illinois in 1883. Within a short time he built up a prosperous business, first contracting with local merchants to deliver goods to their customers, then purchasing the express and transfer service and the Broadway Corral, making the latter his headquarters. By 1884 Jackson had the contract to deliver express goods for Wells, Fargo & Co., running four delivery wagons around the county. He was also local agent for the Las Vegas Ice Company. He established a bus line in Silver City,

running from the hotels and private homes to the depot. Needing larger quarters for his rapidly expanding business, Jackson moved to the Legal Tender Corral on Main Street in 1885 and added a feed and grain store and a wood yard. He opened a machine shop to build and repair machinery of all kinds. In April 1886 Jackson was elected to the town council, but soon afterward sold his Silver City interests and moved to San Jose, California.

13.　On March 11, 1884, the outlaws overpowered their guards and escaped, taking two other prisoners with them. Mounted on horses stolen from the Elephant Corral, they headed north. The hastily organized posse overtook them a few miles from town. In the ensuing gunfight two of the outlaws were killed, one was wounded, two surrendered, and Kit Joy escaped, only to be captured several months later. When the posse discovered that one of their own men, Joe Lafferr, had been killed in the battle, they decided to administer their own brand of frontier justice. A trial was held on the spot. Two of the prisoners were found guilty and immediately hanged from a nearby tree. *The Enterprise,* March 15, 1884.

14.　Joseph N. Lafferr was one of Silver City's most respected citizens. He and his family came to Silver City from Kansas in 1876. His wife died the following year, leaving him with five young children to raise. In addition to mining interests, he sold and repaired sewing machines. He was interested in civic affairs, especially the public school, and served on the school board for a number of years. Lafferr was largely responsible for the erection of the first school house in Silver City, securing the subscriptions and collecting the greater part of the funds required for its construction.

15.　James C. Cooney was Quartermaster Sergeant in the 8th U.S. Cavalry stationed at Fort Bayard. In 1875, while on an exploring expedition in the Mogollon Mountains, he discovered outcroppings rich in silver and copper ore. When Cooney's term of enlistment expired in 1876, he organized a prospecting party and returned to the Mogollons to locate several mining claims. Frequent Apache raids forced the party to abandon their claims. Two years later Cooney and others relocated these claims and began development work. In March 1880 James Cooney was killed in an Indian raid led by Victorio. *Grant County Herald,* March 20, May 8, June 11, 1880.

16.　Michael Cooney was born March 25, 1838, in Durham, Canada. When the Civil War broke out he was living in Chicago and enlisted in the Illinois Volunteer Infantry. After the war he organized the Irish Rifles of the Illinois State Guard and was commissioned a captain. In 1870 Captain Cooney went to New Orleans where he was Inspector of Customs at the time of his brother's death. Within a month he arrived in Silver City to take charge of the Cooney property. *Grant County Herald*, May 29, 1880; *Illustrated History of New Mexico* (1895), pp. 401–5.

17.   Although undeveloped, the Cooney mining property was valued at a quarter of a million dollars in 1880. The most promising claim was the Silver Bar, and Mike Cooney began to push development of this mine. There was no doubt of the richness of the ore, but a large sum of money was needed for machinery and equipment. In the spring of 1883, Mike found financial backing in Iowa, and a mining company was organized. Within a year, $25,000 had been spent, a five-stamp mill erected, a tunnel forty-eight feet long run into the mine, and the company was $65,000 in debt. The property was sold to the Silver Hill Mining Company, and Mike Cooney was appointed superintendent. After three months the new company was $8,000 in debt. Work was suspended and the mine and machinery were leased to Captain Cooney for one year. *Grant County Herald*, March 11, 1882; *Southwest Sentinel*, April 18, Sept. 26, 1883.

18.   The Argo Smelter, near Denver, Colorado, was built in 1878 by the Boston and Colorado Company, who had previously owned a smelter and refinery at Black Hawk, Colorado. They did custom work on Colorado ore and accepted shipments from out-of-state. The process they used enabled the smelter to treat ores containing various elements other than silver and gold. Jerome C. Smiley, *History of Denver*, pp. 551–56.

19.   Mike Cooney's first shipment of ore went to the Argo Smelter in September 1883. From this time through August 1884, when Cooney's lease expired, the Silver Bar is said to have produced a net profit of over $300,000 in spite of the cost of $65 per ton for mining, freighting, and treatment of the ore. Greater reduction facilities were needed, but the stockholders were reluctant to invest more money. The Silver Bar lay idle until 1904 when Thomas F. Cooney, nephew of James and Mike, leased the mine and brought in money for extensive development work. Mike Cooney was elected to the New Mexico Territorial Legislature in 1882 and again in 1888. He served as collector of taxes for Socorro County in 1894. While alone on a prospecting trip in November 1914, he became ill and died of exhaustion and exposure. *The Mogollon Mines*, 1909, pp. 20–21; ibid., 1915, pp. 45–47.

20.   After purchasing the Naiad Queen and other Georgetown mines, the Mimbres Mining Company built a new ten-stamp mill on the river. From this mill and the smaller Meredith and Ailman mill, they were turning out bullion at the rate of $40,000 per month by August 1884. *Silver City Enterprise,* August 24, 1884.

21.   Meredith and Ailman purchased the Georgetown store from G. P. Armstrong in May 1881. Their profit from this store during the first year amounted to $16,000. In December 1882, they sold the business to Meredith's father-in-law, David Bunn, and his associates. *New Southwest,* Dec. 12, 1882; *Grant County Deed Book* 6, pp. 198, 449.

22.   This was the route of the old Spanish trail between Chihuahua, Mexico, and Santa Fe. The road left the Rio Grande at Robledo, passed through the arid *Jornada del Muerto* (journey of the dead man) on the east side of the Fray Christobal Range, and rejoined the river near San Marcos. The only water source along this route was found in two unreliable shallow springs. In the spring of 1871, Jack Martin was successful in sinking a good well about midway along the route. In April he opened a stage station and advertised food and lodging for the traveler. Spencer Wilson, "El Contadero," *Rio Grande History,* No. 6 (1976):6–7; *The Borderer,* April 20, 1871.

23.   The Methodist Church was completed and dedicated in April 1880. It was located on the corner of Broadway and Bayard Streets, one block west of the Ailman residence. Both Episcopalians and Presbyterians held services in the Methodist building until each denomination had its own meeting place.

24.   In addition to the Silver City store and bank, and the Georgetown store, Meredith and Ailman had an interest in the Fort Bayard Post Trader's store, and furnished wholesale merchandise to establish stores in new mining camps. They "grub staked" many prospectors in exchange for an interest in new mineral discoveries.

25.   Jerome Ailman came to Silver City in the summer of 1880, and went to work in the Meredith and Ailman store. The following spring, hoping to benefit his health by a more active life, he joined Ira Smith, Harry's father-in-law, in prospecting and working gold mines at Pinos Altos. He also spent some time helping brothers Herb and Sam at their ranch on the Sapillo. In October 1882, the senior Ailmans came to New Mexico to visit their four sons. In February Jerome accompanied his parents back to Pennsylvania where he resumed his teaching career. He became active in the Pennsylvania State Grange, serving as lecturer

from 1890 to 1894, and as secretary of that organization from 1894 to 1913. Jerome was elected to the Pennsylvania State Legislature for four years in 1908, but was defeated in the race for state senator the following year. *Jerome Ailman Diary*, 1880–1883. A letter in which Jerome describes his stagecoach journey from Albuquerque to Silver City will be found in Appendix B. See also Chapter 5 n.10. Biographical information courtesy Mildred A. Ailman.

26.   Several promising young men were brought from Pennsylvania to work for Meredith and Ailman. John Smith arrived in August 1881, served as cashier for three years, and returned to Pennsylvania. Brodie Crawford arrived, took a look around, and departed on the next stage. Tom Burlan and John McManigil arrived in 1881 to clerk in the Silver City store, and Tom Carson came west the following year to take charge of the Georgetown store. After Meredith and Ailman sold their stores, Burlan, McManigil and Carson went into business for themselves and remained in Grant County many years. *Jerome Ailman Diary*, 1880–1883.

27.   Hamilton Calhoun McComas was a native of Virginia. He practiced law and was active in politics in Illinois, at Fort Scott, Kansas, and at St. Louis, Missouri, before coming to Silver City in 1880. He devoted his time to mining interests until opening a law office in Silver City in 1882. Shortly thereafter he was elected to the Board of Grant County Commissioners, and served as chairman until his death the following year. *Silver City Enterprise*, March 30, 1883.

28.   The McComas party left Silver City March 27, 1883. Their destination was Pyramid City, a mining camp near Lordsburg. They spent the night at Mountain Home, a stage station in the Burro Mountains, and were ambushed the next day just after passing through Thompson's Canyon. When Charley McComas' body was not found, it was supposed that he had been taken captive and carried into Mexico. A reward of $1,000 was offered for his return, or proof of his fate. A year later one of the Apaches who had been on the raid told the authorities that the boy was dead. *Southwest Sentinel*, March 31, 1883; *Silver City Enterprise*, March 28, 1884.

Chapter 7

1.   Leading business men of Silver City began meeting in the summer of 1881 to decide what could be done to run a narrow gauge line from Deming to Silver City. The following March the Silver City,

Deming, and Pacific Railroad was incorporated with capital stock of $600,000. Of this amount, $100,000 had already been subscribed locally, with Meredith and Ailman each pledging $10,000. However, great difficulty was encountered in raising the total amount. In December Boston capitalists took up the remaining stock. The line was completed in March 1883. In July of the next year it was leased to the Santa Fe Railroad who added a third rail to make it standard gauge. The line was sold to the A. T. & S.F. in 1899. James Marshall, *Santa Fe, the Railroad That Built an Empire,* p. 404; *New Southwest,* June 4, 1881; *Southwest Sentinel,* May 10, 1883.

2.   The Golden Rule mine in the Dragoon Mountains of southeastern Arizona was located March 3, 1879, by L. C. Elliott and A. J. Spaulding, and later sold to a group of Silver City men with C. P. Crawford as the principal promoter and stock holder. The Golden Rule appeared to be a very promising prospect. A twenty-stamp mill was erected, and $125,000 in gold was produced the first year. The following year production fell to $30,000 as the high grade ore played out. After the business failure of Crawford, no further work was done on the mine until 1891 when $12,000 worth of ore was shipped to Pinos Altos for refining. After this the mine was worked only intermittently and produced less than $60,000 through 1929. Cochise County, Arizona, *Record of Mines* Book 3, p. 41; Wilson, Cunningham, and Butler, *Arizona Lode Gold Mines and Gold Mining,* p. 121.

3.   The Crawford bank failed in December 1883, just before his new buiilding was completed. At the same time the Grant County Bank, owned by Crawford's father-in-law, Newton Bradley, closed its doors. In March 1884 Henry and Charles Lesinsky, former Silver City merchants who made a sizable fortune from the copper mines at Clifton, Arizona, took over the new Crawford building and opened the Silver City Bank. After a year their depositors were notified to draw out their money because the owners intended to close the bank. This left Meredith and Ailman with the only bank in town.

4.   Max Schutz was born in Essen, Germany, in 1845. He came to America at the age of fifteen aboard a German naval vessel, jumping ship when he reached the United States. He is thought to have joined relatives in the southwest where he learned the mercantile business. Schutz came to Silver City in 1877 and was soon established as one of the leading business men of the area. In 1883 he took over the Meredith and Ailman mercantile store on the corner of Bullard and Broadway.

After Meredith and Ailman went out of business, Schutz purchased the entire building. In 1900, by converting the upstairs into sleeping apartments, he opened the Palace Hotel, with lobby and dining room downstairs and entrance on Broadway. He turned management of the store over to his son, Salo, and nephew, Julius Schwarz in 1904, but remained active in real estate and land development for several years before moving to Los Angeles, California, where he died in 1921.

5. Several large cattle companies were in operation in Grant County by 1884, with extensive grazing lands spreading southward into Mexico. Among the largest of these organizations was the Lyons and Campbell Cattle Company, whose holdings comprised over a million and a half acres of grazing land, and the Victorio Land and Cattle Company owned by George Hearst, James B. Haggin, and A. E. Head. In 1886 the Victorio interests (later known as the Diamond A) reached from the Warm Springs and Apache Tejo ranches, near present-day Hurley, New Mexico, south through the Animas Valley into eastern Arizona and Chihuahua, Mexico, where William Randolph Hearst, son of George, owned a 650,000 acre ranch.

6. In spite of the attempt of the government to boost the economy of the mining industry by the Bland-Allison Act of 1878, the price of silver had continued its steady decline and was down to $1.11 per ounce by 1884. Many of the silver mines around Silver City were closing down because the low-grade ore was not profitable.

7. Jefferson Raynolds was highly regarded as a financier. He was responsible for organizing national banks in Las Vegas, New Mexico, and El Paso, Texas. He also organized the Central Bank of Albuquerque. Following his visit to Silver City, he said,

I am confident Messrs. Meredith and Ailman can do all the banking business your city affords at present, and one good house, properly supported by your citizens, is of more value to the city than half a dozen poorly patronized institutions. If my opinion is worth anything, I would advise a hearty effort on the part of all your citizens to work for Meredith and Ailman, and by building them up you help yourselves, as they are careful and honest men. *Southwest Sentinel,* May 23, 1885.

8. Territorial banking laws in effect in 1885 required private banks to be incorporated by not less than three persons and have capital stock of at least $30,000. The Meredith and Ailman bank did not meet these

requirements, thus the advice to form a national bank was meant to enable them to eventually close out their private bank. *New Mexico Laws,* 1884 Code, Banks and Banking, #142.

9. John Staples Swift amassed a fortune during his business career. He was born in Dublin, Ireland, in 1844. A few years later the Swift family came to America and settled in St. Louis, Missouri. John went to work for the Simmons Hardware Company at the age of thirteen and rose to a position of importance with the firm. Because of severe asthma attacks, he was forced to seek a healthier climate. In 1882 he came to Silver City and opened a hardware store. Ten years later, with his health much improved, he sold his business to Eugene Cosgrove and returned to his home in St. Louis where he died March 7, 1908. *Silver City Enterprise,* March 13, 1908.

10. John R. Brockman was born November 15, 1841, at Hessen, Darmstadt, Germany. At the age of seven he came to the United States with his parents who settled at Rock Island, Illinois. He attended school, worked as a hotel steward, and secured a contract to carry the mail between Rock Island and Loda, Illinois. Following the Civil War, in which he served in the Union Army, Brockman came to New Mexico. He was at Pinos Altos for a short time, then settled on land in the Mimbres Valley. He was appointed deputy collector of customs, opened a general store, erected a grist mill, acquired more'land, and set about improving his herds. By 1885 he had one of the most beautiful and productive ranches in Grant County. *Silver City Enterprise,* April 10, 1925.

11. David Goldman went to work as cashier in the Meredith and Ailman private bank in the summer of 1884, replacing John Smith who returned to Pennsylvania. When the Silver City National Bank was organized, Goldman was appointed cashier. He left Silver City for California in the summer of 1888, joined Meredith in Washington for a time, and then went to Linius, Missouri, where he ran a drug store. Goldman returned to Silver City briefly in 1889 to testify in court regarding the Meredith and Ailman business affairs.

12. The Silver City National Bank was organized with paid up capital of $50,000, most of which was put in by Meredith and Ailman as follows: H. M. Meredith, president, 190 shares—$19,000, paid by Meredith and Ailman; John R. Brockman, vice-president, 190 shares—$19,000, paid by Meredith and Ailman who accepted Brockman's note for this amount; Harry B. Ailman, director, 100 shared—$10,000, paid by Meredith and

Ailman; John Swift, director, 10 shares—$1,000, paid by Swift; and David Goldman, cashier, 10 shares—$1,000, furnished by Meredith and Ailman. They were granted certificate #3539 and opened for business August 16, 1886. *Silver City Enterprise*, August 20, 1886.

13.   Charles H. Dane was born in Lowell, Massachusetts, February 2, 1851. After graduating from Ann Arbor, Michigan, he went to California, was admitted to the bar, and practiced law for five years. When the Southern Pacific Railroad began construction from the Pacific coast, Dane went along as mail and express agent, moving his boxcar office from one construction camp to another as the line progressed toward New Mexico. He took with him a stock of merchandise which he sold for a good profit while en route. Upon reaching Deming, New Mexico, he decided to leave the railroad and go into the furniture business. In April 1881 Dane was appointed postmaster. He founded the Commercial Bank of Deming in 1883, and the following year converted this to the First National Bank of Deming. September 23, 1886, Dane opened the First National Bank of Silver City in the old Grant County Bank building on Main Street. He was active in politics, serving as county treasurer 1886–87, but was defeated for this office the next term by H. M. Meredith. February 3, 1892, both of Dane's banks were closed by order of the U.S. Comptroller of Currency. Dane was indicted by a grand jury and served four years in prison for wrecking the two concerns by the illegal use of their funds to the extent of $181,000. Most of this money went into the promotion of large ranches in Colfax and Sierra Counties.

14.   When the Meredith and Ailman Bank failed, their assets totaled $255,409.73; liabilities were $169,932.18. In addition to valuable Silver City real estate, they owned several mines in the Tres Hermanes and Mogollon districts and shares of stock in active mining companies. They held between $140,000 and $150,000 in notes and mortgages. *Silver City Enterprise*, December 16, 1887.

15.   On the morning of December 8, 1887, the citizens of Silver City found the following notice posted on the door of the Meredith and Ailman Bank:

BANK CLOSED. Notice to depositors. We have been compelled to make an assignment for the benefit of our depositors and creditors. We have not wasted our money in speculation, but have loaned it to residents of our county who

176

have property but no money to pay their notes. Our assignee, George D. Goldman, cashier of the Silver City National Bank, will collect as fast as possible, and we hope, in a reasonable time, will pay all depositors in full. Very respectfully,

Meredith and Ailman

Although some condemned Meredith and Ailman for poor management, there was a general feeling that the depositors would be paid off, as both gentlemen has always been exceedingly economical, and their honesty and integrity had never been questioned. Meredith and Ailman felt that by making an assignment, those who owed the bank money would be given time to pay up; whereas if suits were brought to collect the notes held by the bank, many people would be ruined and businesses destroyed. *Silver City Enterprise,* December 9, 1887.

16.   Thomas F. Conway was born in St. Louis, Missouri, in 1835. He graduated from Missouri State University along with Steven B. Elkin, Thomas B. Catron, and H. S. Waldo. These prominent New Mexico politicians may have been responsible for Conway coming to Santa Fe in the early 1860s. He began the practice of law in the office of Judge Ashurst in 1865, and a few years later opened his own office with John Risque. Conway was appoinited United States Attorney for the Territory of New Mexico upon the resignatoin of Thomas Catron in 1872. Two years later the firm of Conway and Risque opened a branch office in Silver City. Risque managed this office until he was killed by Apaches in 1882, at which time Conway closed the Santa Fe office and moved to Silver City. Conway was described as quiet and distinguished—said to prefer the fireside to the forum. He was one of the most popular members of the bar. For many years he was the personal attorney for John Chisum. Thomas Conway died in Silver City January 7, 1900. *Silver City Enterprise,* January 12, 1900.

17.   In making an assignment in a business failure, assets were turned over to an assignee to be held in trust for the creditors and debts paid off as property was sold, notes collected, and so forth. Designating certain people as preferred creditors meant that their accounts would be settled first, leaving fewer assets to be divided among the remaining creditors.

18.   Thirty-six suits were immediately brought against Meredith and Ailman to break the assignment. A court order was issued freezing funds and preventing sale of property. The estate became entangled in so much litigation that it took four years to straighten it out. When the cases

first came to trial, a change of venue was asked to remove them from local prejudice. At the next session of court, December 1888, in Las Cruces, the jury was unable to reach a verdict, and the cases were carried over to the next term. Again a change of venue was sought, and the trial was transferred to Hillsboro, Sierra County. Here the jury ruled that the assignment was fraudulent. Max Schutz and John Brockman, as preferred creditors, decided to carry the case to the supreme court. It was agreed by all parties that the suit of Harry W. Elliott against Meredith and Ailman would be the test case. Finally, January 1891, the supreme court upheld the decision of the lower court. The receiver was ordered to collect all money due the estate and deposit it in a special account at the First National Bank of Santa Fe from which creditors would be paid.

19.   At the time of the bank failure, Meredith, as county treasurer, was responsible for over sixteen thousand dollars in county funds on deposit with the Meredith and Ailman Bank. The Grant County Commissioners immediately demanded Meredith's resignation. As this would require him to turn over all county funds to his successor, Meredith refused to resign. The commissioners had him arrested on charges of misappropriating county funds. They later agreed to accept Meredith's note for the amount due, to be paid off by the receiver as money was available, and the charges were dropped. Meredith was in poor health and had received a number of letters threatening his life. In the summer of 1888 he moved his family to the state of Washington, leaving Ailman in Silver City to do what he could to straighten out their tangled affairs. Even though his testimony was needed, he wrote several letters to Ailman in which he stated that he did not want to return for fear of being molested or detained. Personal Letters, Meredith to Ailman, February 17, April 10, May 5, September 14, October 26, 1890.

20.   W. A. Leonard came to Silver City from Santa Fe where he had been connected with the newspaper, *The New Mexican.* He founded the *Silver City Enterprise,* bringing out the first issue October 25, 1882. He was also interested in mining and ranching, started an angora goat ranch north of town and organized the Enterprise Cattle Company. Leonard sold the *Enterprise* in 1893 and moved to Velasco, Texas, where he founded the *Velasco Times.* He later went to California, then returned to Texas where he published the *Angelton Times* for several years. In 1901 he moved to Arizona and became editor of the *Clifton Copper Era.*

21.   The reason for Ailman's bitterness toward former business asso-

ciate John Brockman is revealed by the court records. Brockman was claiming full ownershop of the bank building and certain other property that had been purchased jointly with Meredith and Ailman. He also appears to have transferred Meredith and Ailman's Silver City National Bank stock to his own name shortly after their business failed, claiming to have purchased said stock. Through his agent, D. C. Hobart, Brockman had quietly bought up $65,000 worth of claims and liens against Meredith and Ailman, and filed suit to collect his money from the estate. W. A. Leonard, as receiver for the estate, countered with suits against Brockman to recover these valuable assets which were needed to pay off debts of Meredith and Ailman. The cases went to court December 1890, and Meredith returned from Washington to testify. With the approval of the court, a compromise agreement was finally reached in July 1891. Meredith and Ailman gave up their interest in the jointly owned property in payment of some of the claims held by Brockman. Brockman was ordered by the court to return the bank stock or pay Meredith and Ailman $24,000. From this amount Meredith and Ailman were to pay off $13,000 in additional claims owed to Brockman and the Silver City National Bank. This left a balance of $11,000 to be divided among the remaining creditors. When the Broadway Street property was sold at public auction in 1892, the Ailman house was purchased by Brockman's agent, D. C. Hobart for $3,500; the Meredith house went to his lawyer, G. D. Bantz, for $2,343; and Brockman purchased a large brick warehouse at the rear of the property for $2,251. *Third Judicial District Court,* Dockets 2169, 2302, 2303, 2380; *Grant County Deed Records,* Book 26, pp. 449–61.

22.   In March 1892 Brockman promoted the sale of valuable iron deposits in Hanover Gulch to a group of Philadelphia capitalists. The Hanover-Bessemer Iron Association was organized, and for years this company supplied iron ore to the Colorado Fuel and Iron Company at Pueblo, Colorado.

23.   In July 1894 Brockman leased several supposedly valuable gold mines in the White Signal district, south of Silver City. He formed a company with Richard Penrose and D. C. Barringer, Colorado mining engineers, to develop the property. They erected a mill which proved a failure because sufficient water was not available to operate it. The ore taken from the mines was also a disappointment, and in October of that same year operations were suspended.

24.   The Commonwealth mine, located about 125 miles northeast

of Tombstone, Arizona, was discovered by Jimmy Pearce in 1894. The first carload of ore shipped to El Paso assayed at eighty dollars silver and twenty dollars gold per ton. Brockman is said to have paid $10,000 for a ninety-day option on the mine. Within sixty days he had stockpiled more than this amount of ore. Brockman, Richard Penrose, and D. C. Barringer, backed by Philadelphia capital, organized the Commonwealth Mining and Milling Company, with Penrose as president and Brockman as general manager. The mine was purchased for $250,000. Brockman took possesion for the company in the spring of 1896 and began construction of a 200-stamp mill. From 1900 to 1903, when the mine was sold, the owners are said to have netted more than $3,000,000 annually. Press Reference Library (Western Edition), *Notables of the West,* Vol. 2, p. 136–37.

25. John Brockman and his family left Silver City in 1896 and established their home in Los Angeles, California. Brockman continued as general manager of the Commonwealth Company until 1910, investing his money in commercial property in downtown Los Angeles as well as ranches and real estate around southern California. His palatial home, surrounded by beautifully landscaped grounds, was situated on a hundred-acre estate in Glendale, He died of pneumonia, March 29, 1925, at the age of eighty-five. *Silver City Independent,* March 31, 1925.

26. In November 1888, H. M. Meredith and his family left Silver City and went to the territory of Washington. He sold life insurance for a time and was employed by a Boston company to investigate and report on iron and coal deposits at Hamilton, in the Skagit River country. In 1889, he and his father-in-law, David Bunn, opened a brickyard in Seattle. A fire had demolished much of the city, creating a great demand for building materials. They sold the brickyard in the spring of 1890 and bought a farm at Sultan City, sixty miles north of Seattle and near a new silver mining region. Meredith and Bunn farmed, prospected, and built a river steamer which they operated on the Skykomish River until the railroad was built in 1892. Meredith formed a partnership with Tom W. Cobb, fomerly of Silver City, to open a general mercantile store in Sultan City. This business failed in a short time, leaving Meredith practically penniless. In 1893 he received the appointment of commissioner of the U.S. circuit court and postmaster of Sultan. Unable to purchase post office fixtures, valued at sixty dollars, he gave his note for that amount and borrowed forty dollars to buy a small stock of cigars and tobacco to sell in the office. With long hours and hard work,

Meredith's business prospered. He opened a sawmill east of town and was one of the organizers of a commercial fishing company. He continued to be interested in civic affairs and active in politics. When Sultan City was incorporated, in 1905, Meredith was unanimously elected its first mayor. He died of cancer, January 6, 1907, at the age of sixty-six. *An Illustrated History of Skagit and Snohomish Counties,* pp. 1098–99; *Silver City Independent,* January 22, 1907.

Bibliography

Books

Appleton's Cyclopaedia of American Biography, ed. by James Grant Wilson and John Fiske, 6 vols., New York: D. Appleton and Company, 1898.

Bell, William A. *New Tracks in North America: A Journal of Travel and Adventure Whilst Engaged in the Survey for a Southern Railroad to the Pacific Ocean During 1867–1868.* Albuquerque: Horn and Wallace, 1965.

Callon, Millon W. *Las Vegas, New Mexico: The Town That Wouldn't Gamble.* Las Vegas: Las Vegas Publishing Company, Inc., 1962.

Carter, Harvey Lewis. *Dear Old Kit: The Historical Christopher Carson.* Norman: University of Oklahoma Press, 1968.

Colyer, Vincent. *Peace With the Apaches of New Mexico and Arizona.* Washington: Government Printing Office, 1872. (Reprinted as *Report on the Apache Indians of Arizona and New Mexico.* Tucson: Arizona Silhouettes, 1964.)

Dick, Everett. *Vanguards of the Frontier.* Lincoln: University of Nebraska Press, 1941.

Dils, Lenore. *Horny Toad Man.* El Paso: Boots and Saddle Press, 1966.

Dunning, Charles H. with Edward H. Peplow, Jr., *Rock to Riches: The Story of American Mining . . . Past, Present and Future . . . as reflected in the colorful History of Mining in Arizona, The Nation's Greatest Bonanza.* Pasadena: Hicks Publishing Corporation, 1966.

Emmett, Chris. *Fort Union and the Winning of the Southwest.* Norman: University of Oklahoma Press, 1965.

Frazer, Robert W. *Forts of the West: Military Forts and Presidios and Posts*

Commonly Called Forts West of the Mississippi River to 1898. Norman: University of Oklahoma Press, 1965.

Grinstead, Marion C. *Life and Death of a Frontier Fort: Fort Craig, New Mexico 1854–1885.* Socorro: Socorro County Historical Society, 1973.

Hammond, George P. *The Adventures of Alexander Barclay, Mountain Man: From London Corsetier to Pioneer Farmer in Canada, Bookkeeper in St. Louis, Supt. of Bent's Fort, Fur Trader & Mt. Man in Colorado and New Mexico, Builder of Barclay's Fort on the Santa Fe Trail, New Mexico in 1848.* Denver: Old West Publishing Company, 1976.

Hodge, Frederick Webb, ed. *Handbook of American Indians North of Mexico.* Smithsonian Institution Bureau of American Ethnology, Bulletin 30. Washington: Government Printing Office, 1912.

Holbrook, Stewart H. *The Story of American Railroads.* New York: Crown (Bonanza), 1947.

Huning, Franz. *Trader on the Santa Fe Trail: Memoirs of Franz Huning,* with notes by his grandaughter Lina Fergusson Browne. Albuquerque: University of Albuquerque with Calvin Horn Publisher, Inc., 1973.

Illustrated History of New Mexico. Chicago: Lewis Publishing Company, 1895.

An Illustrated History of Skagit and Snohomish Counties. (Washington) Interstate Publishing Company, 1906.

Lange, Charles H., and Carroll L. Riley, eds. *The Southwestern Journals of Adolph F. Bandelier, 1880–1882.* Albuquerque: Univeristy of New Mexico Press, 1966.

——— *The Southwestern Journals of Adolph F. Bandelier, 1883–1884.* Albuquerque: University of New Mexico Press, 1970.

Lasky, S.G. and T.P. Wooton. *The Metal Resources of New Mexico and Their Economic Features.* State Bureau of Mines and Mineral Resources Bulletin #7. Socorro: New Mexico School of Mines, 1933.

Marshall, James. *Santa Fe: The Railroad That Built an Empire.* New York: Random House, 1945.

Meline, James F. *Two Thousand Miles on Horseback: Santa Fe and Back; a Summer Tour Through Kansas, Nebraska, Colorado, and New Mexico in the Year 1866.* Albuquerque: Horn & Wallace, 1966.

Morris, Richard B., ed. *Encyclopedia of American History.* New York: Harper & Row, 1976.

Morrison, R.S. *Mining Rights in the Western States and Territories: Lode and Placer Claims, Possessory and Patented; Statutes, Land Office and Surveyor General's Rules: Instructions to Prospectors, Locators, Convey-*

ancers, Incorporators and Surveyors, with Forms, Decisions, etc. Denver: The Chain and Hardy Company, 8th ed., 1895.

Muelberger, William R., Brewster Baldwin, and Roy W. Foster. *High Plains Northeastern New Mexico.* Scenic Trips to the Geologic Past #7. Socorro: New Mexico Institute of Mining and Technology, 1967.

New Mexico: A Guide to the Colorful State, compiled by Workers of the Writers' Program of the Work Projects Administration in the State of New Mexico. American Guide Series. New York: Hastings House, 1940.

Oliva, Leo E. *Soldiers on the Santa Fe Trail.* Norman: University of Oklahoma Press, 1967.

Paul, Rodman Wilson. *Mining Frontiers of Far West 1848–1880,* Histories of the American Frontier Series. New York: Holt, Rinehart & Winston, Inc., 1963.

Pearce, T.M. *New Mexico Place Names.* Albuquerque: University of New Mexico Press, 1965.

Pierce, Benjamin E. *Memories of Pierces in Parsonages.* Published by the author, 1975.

Pike, Zebulon Montgomery. *The Journals of Zebulon Montgomery Pike,* edited and annotated by Donald Jackson. Norman: University of Oklahoma, 1966.

Press Reference Library (Western Edition). *Notables of the West.* New York: International News Service, 1915.

Raymond, Rossiter W. *Statistics of Mines and Mining in the States and Territories West of the Rocky Mountains.* 41st Congress, 2d session, House of Representatives, Ex. Document #207. Washington: G.P.O., 1870.

———— *Statistics of Mines and Mining in the States and Territories West of the Rocky Mountains: being the fifth annual report of Rossiter W. Raymond, U.S. Commissioner of Mining Statistics.* 42nd Congress, 3d session, House of Representatives, Ex. Document #210. Washington: G.P.O., 1873.

Riddle, Kenyon. *Records and Maps of the Old Santa Fe Trail,* edited by John Riddle and Nancy Riddle Madden. Stuart (Fla.): Southeastern Printing Co., 1963.

Riegel, Robert Edgar. *The Story of Western Railroads.* New York: Macmillan Co., 1926. (Lincoln: University of Nebraska Press, 1967.)

Russell, Don. *The Lives and Legends of Buffalo Bill.* Norman: University of Oklahoma Press, 1960.

Schmitt, Martin F., ed. *General George Crook: His Autobiography.* Norman: University of Oklahoma Press, 1960.

184

Bibliography

Stratton, David H., ed. *The Memoirs of Albert B. Fall.* Southwestern Studies, Monograph #15. El Paso: Texas Western Press, 1966.

Smiley, Jerome C. *History of Denver with Outlines of the Rocky Mountain Country.* Denver: The Denver Times-Times/Dun Publishing Co., 1901.

Taylor, Morris F. *First Mail West.* Albuquerque: University of New Mexico, 1971.

Twitchell, Ralph Emerson. *The Leading Facts of New Mexican History.* Albuquerque: Horn & Wallace, 1963.

Wilson, Eldred D., J.B. Cunningham, and G.M. Butler. *Arizona Lode Gold Mines and Gold Mining.* Arizona Bureau of Mines, Mineral Technology Series #37, Bulletin #137. Tucson: University of Arizona, 1934.

Newspapers

The Daily Southwest (Silver City)
The Grant County Herald (Silver City)
Mining Life (Silver City)
Silver City Enterprise
Southwest Sentinel (Silver City)
The Tribune (Silver City)
The Borderer (Las Cruces)
Mogollon Mines
Rocky Mountain News (Denver)
Santa Fe Weekly New Mexican
Weekly New Mexican (Santa Fe)

Periodicals

Bloom, Lansing B., ed. "Bourke on the Southwest, II," *New Mexico Historical Review,* 9(January 1934):33–77.

Cannon, Julia Brannin. "Silver Boom Town," *New Mexico Magazine,* 29(July 1951):23, 45, 47

Fierman, Floyd S., ed. "Nathan Bibo's Reminiscences of Early New Mexico," *El Palacio,* 68(1961):231–57; 69(1961):40–60.

Jenkins, Myra Ellen. "The Baltasar Baca 'Grant,' History of an Encroachment," *El Palacio,* 68(1961):47–63.

Myers, Lee. "Military Establishments in Southwestern New Mexico: Stepping Stones to Settlement," *New Mexico Historical Review,* 43(1968): 5–48.

Reeve, Frank D., ed. "Frederick E. Phelps: A Soldier's Memoirs," *New Mexico Historical Review,* 25(1950):37–56, 109–35, 187–221, 305–27.

Rickard, T.A. "The Chino Enterprise," *Engineering & Mining Journal-Press,* 116(1923):753–58, 803–10, 981–85, 1113–21; 117(1924): 13–20.

Ruhlen, George. "Kearney's Route from the Rio Grande to the Gila River," *New Mexico Historical Review,* 32(1957):213–30.

Scott, P.G. "Diary of a Freighting Trip from Kit Carson to Trinidad in 1870," *The Colorado Magazine,* 8(1931):146–54.

Seldon, H.D. "Territorial Post Office of New Mexico," *New Mexico Historical Review,* 33(1958):322–27; 34(1959):55–69, 145–52, 203–26, 308–9.

Shouse, Betty. "Anton Chico, Historic Village," *New Mexico Magazine,* 37 (1959):3–6.

Wilson, Spencer, "El Contadero," *Rio Grande History,* 6(1976):6–7.

Public Records

Second U.S. Census, 1800, Newport County, Rhode Island, Reel M32, #46.

Grant County, New Mexico—Record of Deeds, Books 1, 2, 3.

—————— Mining Record of Deeds, Book 18.

—————— District Court Docket, 3rd Judicial District, 1887–1892.

Cochise County, Arizona—Record of Mines, Book 3.

New Mexico Laws, 1884 Code, Banks and Banking, #142.

Personal Papers

Diaries of Harry B. Ailman
  "Sketch of My Arizona Trip", March 5, 1871—September 3, 1871
  "Trip to Mexico", October 27, 1891—December 3, 1891

Letters—H.M. Meredith to Harry B. Ailman, February 17, 1890; April 10, 1890; May 5, 1890; September 14, 1890, October 26, 1890.

Diary of Jerome Ailman, April 30, 1880 to March 2, 1883

Letter—E. E. Burlingame, Silver City, to Alice Hoffamn, Central City, Colorado, June 6, 1873.

Unpublished Material

Berry, Susan, *Survey of Historical Buildings in Silver City,* 1979.
Milliken, Marie Stevens, *Isaac James Stevens, His Experience As a Pioneer.*
Unpublished manuscript courtesy of Myrtle Whitehill Carlisle, Deming, New Mexico.

Index

Roach, Thomas, 47
Robb, John, 4
robbery, 63, 70
Robbin, Stephen P., 12–13, 18, 39
Rocky Mountains, 6, 17, 119
ruins, 57–58, 110, 126, 127

Sabbath, 16
Sabinal, 116
St. Cyr, Ben, 64
St. Louis, 52, 75, 77, 78, 108
San Diego, 37
San Francisco, 37, 38
San Marcial, 32
San Pablo mine, 127
San Pedro mine, 127
San Simon Cattle Company, 122–23
San Simon River, 123
Santa Fe (N.M.), 34, 51
Santa Fe Railroad, 67, 70, 74, 75
Santa Rita, 44, 47, 54, 77, 101
Santa Rita copper mine, xiii, 34, 56, 111
Santa Rita Mountain, 110
scarlet fever, 109–10
Schutz, Max, 97, 99
Sheep's Springs, 21
Sierra County, 66, 100
Sierra Blanca Mountains, 22, 26
Sierra Madre Mountains, 122
Silver City, xiii, 27, 34, 35, 37, 49, 53, 54, 55, 59, 67–101, 107, 110, 113–14, 115, 120, 121, 128, 130; reputation, 38–39
Silver City Enterprise, 107

Silver City, Deming, and Pacific Railroad, 96
Silver City National Bank, 98–100
Silver: market, 50, 97, 107, 111, 113, 130–31; mining, xiii, 61, 67, 71, 77, 96, 102, 111; important industry, 50
Silver Purchase Law, 97, 131
Slaughter, John, 123–24
smelting, 32, 38–39, 43–44, 46, 72, 101
Smith, Ira E., 56, 57, 58, 102
Smith, John, 76
Smith, Luthera, 110
Smith, P. W., 125, 129
Smith, Virginia, 56, 58
Smithsonian Institution, 58
Snohomish, 100
Snyder County (Pa.), 1
Socorro, 32, 34, 69, 74, 116
Sonora, 70
Southern Pacific Railroad, 63, 67, 70, 75, 77, 122
Spanish Mountains, 19
Spillar, John, 51, 54
stage coaches, 51, 74, 75, 76, 115–21
Stein's Pass, 122
Stevens, Isaac, 67
Swift, John S., 97

Tennessee Mill, 53
Thomas, William B., 29
Tipton, W. B., 19
Topeka, 12
Transportation, 74–75, 96; of merchandise, 68–69; of ore,